Devotions for Every Day of the Year

-Tanya Glessner-

New Mercies Every Morning

Find more books, resources, and personal blogs by

Tanya Glessner:

www.tanyaglessner.com

January

January 1

Jeremiah 29:11

Before you were born, God knew exactly what His plans were for you. He knew every mistake that you would ever make, every tear that you would ever cry, and every obstacle that you would be faced with. Above all, He knew His presence would be there with you through all of it.

We often find ourselves questioning what God is doing and where He is in the midst of our suffering, but God never promised we wouldn't have hardships. God does promise us however, that whatever struggle we are going through, He will use it for good for those who seek Him. Just look at the example of Jesus Christ and the sufferings He endured before being glorified.

We must ask ourselves if we are agreeing with God's plan for our lives, or if we're fighting for the steering wheel trying to speed off in our own direction. Our plans may look good, but what God has planned is always immeasurably greater. God gave us the gift of knowing His will through the Bible, and we can measure every choice we make by seeking out what God has to say about it through His word.

We are temples of the Most High God, so whenever you feel that you can't go on, remember that all you ever need is already within you.

January 2

Deuteronomy 1:29

The Bible repeatedly instructs us to not be afraid and recounts many stories of people who turned to the Lord, drawing strength from Him to confront their fears and prevail over them.

God knew humanity in its fallen state would grapple with earthly fears like anxiety, worry, doubt, and discouragement. Relying solely on our own limited understanding, rather than divine wisdom, fosters these fears and leaves no room for reverent awe of God.

When we develop a reverent fear of God that supersedes worldly fears, we gain access to peace, hope, confidence, and assurance that empower us to face every challenge. This godly fear allows the transcendent peace of God to permeate our hearts.

Fearing God means honoring, loving, trusting, and respecting Him. We can nurture these virtues by immersing ourselves in His word, thereby deepening our understanding of His nature. We must relinquish control and have faith in God's plan.

With great love, God casts out all fear. His perfect love assures us that no matter what happens here on Earth, the glory of Heaven awaits.

January 3

Joshua 23:14

This scripture provides a reassuring reminder of God's enduring faithfulness. God remains unchanging - "the same yesterday, today and always." We can take comfort in knowing that God does not waver or reverse His promises. When God speaks, His word stands eternal and unaltered.

Each morning, we can wake up with confidence praising God for fulfilling His promises. However, this does not always mean He will answer our requests as we hope. As we navigate life's storms, we must maintain faith that our merciful God will deliver us.

God's promises remind us of our need for Him. Our future depends on faith and obedience. We can follow the world or follow the Lord. Whatever we choose, God remains faithful, loving us each step of the journey.

When storms arise and you find yourself focusing on the difficulties, take a moment to reflect with gratitude on the blessings God has given you and how He has supported you through each hardship.

Jesus has gone before us and prepared a place for us in Heaven. All we must do is follow Him.

January 4

Esther 4:14

You were created with a unique purpose that only you can fulfill in your own distinctive way. God chose you, designated you, and equipped you with everything you need to accomplish that purpose.

You are right where you are meant to be at this moment. Every experience you have overcome has uniquely prepared you for the next chapter of your life. God has called on you to remain faithful in your current circumstances.

Embracing God's call may present difficulties in the face of overwhelming opposition, yet it is vital to acknowledge the omnipotence of our God. Succumbing to fear over faith may result in us forfeiting significant blessings.

Though God can accomplish His purposes without us, He knows our faith grows stronger with each victory we experience when answering His call. By responding to God's invitation, we discover our identity in Him, His power in us, and the purpose for our unique position at this moment in time.

If you feel called by God to a purpose, have faith that God will guide you through any challenges along the way.

Job 1:21

Even if we give our all, life can still present challenges. During these tough times, it is important to keep praising God and relying on His grace. Although our faith may be tested, God uses these trials to foster our spiritual growth.

The story of Job epitomizes both tragedy and inspiration. Despite losing everything, Job responded to his plight with astounding faith and loyalty, bowing in humble reverence to praise God amidst the storm.

Jesus cautioned that we would face difficulties in this world, yet also assured us of triumph through Him. Job prevailed because he trusted that God controlled all circumstances, whether favorable or adverse.

Job's unwavering devotion to God, even in the midst of trials and tribulations, ultimately thwarted Satan's attempts to undermine his faith. This resulted in Satan being left defeated and silenced, unable to shake Job's steadfast commitment to his Creator.

Our response to suffering is crucial. Suffering can be an instrument to draw us nearer to God, allowing us to recognize our reliance upon Him. Take comfort in knowing that God can create beauty from pain.

January 6

Philippians 1:6

Every born-again believer is continuously being transformed to reflect the image of Jesus Christ. God works with care, patience, and purpose to thoroughly shape believers into Christ's likeness.

By the grace of God and through faith, you have been saved. Through Christ, you have been sanctified, chosen, and forgiven of all wrongdoing. As we surrender to the guidance of the Lord, the fruits of the spirit begin to manifest in our daily lives.

Even though we may face challenges along the way, as we hold onto our faith in the Lord, our journey with Him becomes more stable.

Instead of losing hope in yourself, know that God still believes in you. Every new day brings a chance to enhance and develop. Through the distinctive experiences in life, the Lord molds us into the individuals He always meant us to become.

This journey isn't about you. It's about the work God has begun in you and will continue until the day of Jesus Christ's return. God has a perfect plan for your life—one far greater than any you could imagine.

Thanks be to our rock who is able to keep us from falling.

January 7

Ephesians 3:12

It is a blessing to belong to God's family. Through Jesus Christ, we can boldly and confidently approach God's throne.

When God gazes upon you, He sees the redemption brought by Jesus' sacrifice. You are a beloved child of God, forgiven, cherished, and lifted up. The gates of God's Kingdom are wide open for you.

God yearns for closeness with us. He longs to listen as we share the joys and troubles of our days, unburdening the heaviness in our hearts.

Prayer deepens our relationship with God and lifts the weight from our shoulders, allowing us to fully rely on our Savior.

This scripture is also a comforting reminder that no matter where we are, no matter how dire our circumstances may be, we have an all-powerful God that we have unlimited access to.

Praise and gratitude are due to our extraordinary Redeemer, as the gateway to paradise has been unlocked, bestowing upon us immediate entry to the divine presence of God. With utmost warmth and affection, your loving Father eagerly anticipates your arrival.

January 8

Genesis 1:1

The universe and everything in it exist because of our Creator, who fashioned all things into being. With a word, God brought creation out of nothingness, demonstrating divine power. Reflecting on God's ability to create existence from void inspires awe at what God can accomplish in our lives.

Though King David committed grave sins of adultery and murder, he repented genuinely, and God still used him in mighty ways to bring glory and honor to His name.

Originally a Pharisee who persecuted Christians, Apostle Paul radically transformed after encountering God on the road to Damascus, repenting of his former ways. God then powerfully used Paul to teach, write, and inspire countless believers.

The Bible contains many accounts of individuals regarded as wicked or immoral who, through divine intervention, went on to profoundly influence God's Kingdom.

Our Creator can transform brokenness into beauty, chaos into order, and nothing into something. This should fill us with awe and wonder at what God is capable of, leaving no doubt that no one is beyond redemption.

January 9

Leviticus 26:13

When God declares you as a new creation, it is a definitive statement! You have undergone a complete rebirth and transformation. The previous version of yourself has vanished, making way for a fresh identity.

The worldly labels that once defined you no longer hold any significance. Instead, God has bestowed upon you new designations like chosen, royal, forgiven, loved, and saved. With heads held high, we can walk in God's light, embracing His grace and glory.

You've made it this far because of God's grace, and He won't leave you now. God will continue to work in you, love you, and lead you. We're all works in progress, moving forward with God's strength, until we achieve perfection when Jesus returns.

Don’t be hard on yourself. Shame and guilt are lies from the enemy meant to distract you from the new life and purpose God has given you. If God no longer remembers our sins, why should we dwell on them?

We are no longer bound by our past; as children of God Most High, we are now liberated. The chains that once bound us have been shattered, granting us freedom.

January 10

Exodus 20:8-11

It's easy to get overwhelmed by the daily hustle and bustle, with each day bringing its own demanding to-do list. By the time the weekend arrives, our unfinished tasks and hectic schedules can encroach on what little free time we have left.

When God went to work creating, He mapped out a seven-day plan. The first six days He labored creating our earthly home, and on the seventh day He rested. God took time to sit back and enjoy the fruits of His labor.

The Sabbath honors God as a holy day set apart for communion with Him. The first six days are spent pouring ourselves into work, while the seventh allows for rejuvenating both body and soul.

If your work schedule does not permit observing a traditional Sabbath day of rest, you can still honor this holy day by incorporating Sabbath practices into your weekly routine.

Consider watching an online church service, reading scripture, doing a digital detox with family, spending time in nature, praying, connecting with other believers, or simply resting - whatever allows you to be present with God.

January 11

2 Kings 7:9

Have you ever been on the verge of giving up because your situation looked utterly hopeless? Only to realize down the road that God had it handled long before your first anxious thought. And not only did He have it handled, but He also placed unimaginable blessings on your path.

When something welcome and unexpected happens, our first instinct is to share the good news with loved ones. The news may seem too good to be true, but it serves as proof that everything unfolds according to God's plan.

When you find yourself blind to hope, turn to the one who has proven Himself faithful. Your loving Father will work all things for your good just as He promised.

It's in these dark times that we can find our deepest joy in Him. Loving the giver above the gifts allows us to experience joy through the knowledge of God despite our circumstances.

We can find hope as we shift our gaze from our worldly view to His omnipotent presence. God is able to do immeasurably more than we can ask or imagine. Spend some quiet time alone with Him and allow Jesus to be the antidepressant for your soul.

January 12

Ephesians 6:13

When a baseball catcher takes their place on the baseball field, you will notice that they have several pieces of very important equipment covering their bodies.

They are aware of the dangers that may come their way as they man their position on the field. A catcher is adorned with a mitt, mask, chest protector, as well as shin and knee guards. Even though their eye is always on the ball, they know accidents happen.

We should start each day by spiritually preparing ourselves, because our true battles are not against flesh and blood, but against the evil spiritual forces that rule the darkness in this world.

God instructs us to stand resolute, equipped with the belt of truth, the breastplate of righteousness, feet ready with the gospel of peace, the shield of faith to deflect attacks seeking to destroy, the helmet of salvation, and the sword of the Spirit—God's word.

We have been given honored positions in God's spiritual army. Rather than fight the enemy by our own power, we are meant to draw on the power of our Lord Jesus Christ, who has equipped us with everything needed for victory.

January 13

Romans 12:13

As children of our Heavenly Father, we have a responsibility to care for one another. We ought to check on our elderly members and those who are ill or in need.

As the world observes us, we must exemplify the values of our Lord Jesus Christ so that others see His light reflected through our actions. We are called not only to serve each other but also to look after the needs of our enemies.

As a family gifted with diverse spiritual talents, when we each contribute our share, we can meet any need that arises. As Christians, we should love and support each other and strive to bring others to salvation.

We can meet the needs of those around us through financial generosity or hospitality. In biblical times, followers sold their lands and possessions to meet others' needs. They opened their homes and hearts to complete strangers. How often do you see that happening in the world today?

Rather than buying your 50th pair of shoes, consider using that money to buy a pair for someone who only owns one. You could also invite someone over for coffee and prayer, sharing in fellowship together.

January 14

Luke 6:31

How many times throughout your life have you witnessed your enemy falling on hard times? Maybe their spouse left them, maybe they lost their job, or wrecked their brand-new car?

Did you find that your heart was drawn to compassion for them? Or did you feel a sense of satisfaction? Maybe a little of both? Now imagine that it was you facing these hard times in the presence of your enemy. How would you want them to treat you?

God calls us to treat others with kindness, even if they have mistreated us in the past. We can use these opportunities to show the compassion of Jesus and rise above our sinful tendencies when facing our enemies and all those around us.

Though showing kindness in an unkind world is challenging, we must not expect reciprocation when extending grace to the undeserving. There will be times when kindness feels impossible, but remember the grace the Lord has given you.

The next time you encounter your enemy, surprise them with a random act of kindness. Consider smiling and opening the door for them, bringing them a cup of coffee, or asking them if you can pray for them, and watch God go to work!

January 15

John 10:27-28

As the sheep Jesus refers to in this scripture, we belong to the Lord once we have surrendered our lives to Him. We seek His voice in every scripture we read and church service we attend, welcoming Him into our hearts where others have rejected Him.

In the second part of this scripture, Jesus clearly states that not only do we belong to Him, but that we have eternal life, and no one can take us away from Him. This also demonstrates our need for a Shepherd.

Jesus died once for all, serving as the sole bridge that we must cross to reach Heaven. We are blessed with the Holy Spirit dwelling within us, providing guidance throughout life's journey.

The world today is filled with a cacophony of voices competing for our attention, from the endless promotion of television shows to social media's relentless peddling of the latest ideologies.

Though we all stray at times, there is a caring Shepherd guiding us tenderly to our eternal home. He attends to our every need and shields us from harm. Be encouraged - you are loved with an endless love and called by name.

January 16

Acts 3:19

When someone we love hurts us, we hope they will recognize their mistake, sincerely apologize, and demonstrate through future actions that they meant it. Rather than just wanting an apology, we hope for changed behavior proving their remorse was real.

To truly repent means acknowledging that our ways are wrong, and that we are willing to back up this admission of our transgressions with actions that support corrected behavior.

We have all felt the hurt that comes from broken promises and empty apologies. Forgiveness stays out of reach when wrongs happen over and over, with a countless series of broken vows. We need to put aside our pride, humble ourselves, and admit our wrongs.

God calls us to turn back to Him, confess our sins, and live righteously when we seek true forgiveness. He promises that by doing so, our transgressions will be blotted out as if they never occurred.

As you journey through life, you will stumble at times. Though you may not always get it right, the Lord will be by your side, with an outstretched hand to help you up when you fall.

January 17

1 Corinthians 6:19-20

When the Holy Spirit takes up residence within us, we are to treat our bodies as a sacred temple belonging to the Lord our God. This means giving up toxic things such as alcohol, drugs, and sexual promiscuity.

It's natural to want to have fun in life. Yet some choices can carry heavy risks we may overlook in the moment, like substance abuse or unsafe sex. I gently ask you to pause and consider - is a fleeting high, or brief sexual encounter worth the potential harm to your health and future?

Small compromises lead down a slippery slope toward serious consequences. We may be tempted to tell ourselves, "I'll just do it one time." However, even a single lapse in judgment can put us in an irreversible situation that we deeply regret.

When we empty ourselves of a bad behavior, we must fill the void with a healthier option; although this may feel uncomfortable at first, the more we intentionally choose healthier behaviors, the more natural and rewarding they become over time.

As you go about your day, remind yourself that your body is a sacred space, worthy of only the best.

January 18

1 Samuel 2:9

Although we may strive with all our heart, resources, and power to achieve our deepest desires, if the Lord does not will it, our efforts will ultimately be in vain. In fact, if our desires are not aligned with the Lord's will, God will thwart our plans entirely.

As we start living according to God's word, we understand that we can bring all our prayers to Him, knowing He will grant the desires of our heart if they align with His plan and His perfect timing. We serve an awesome God who can turn impossible situations into miraculous blessings.

God's words, when we internalize them, guide us like a lamp lighting our path, led by the Holy Spirit to keep us from stumbling as we walk through life. We as believers have the honor of rejoicing in the Lord's light, but those who do not believe will remain lost in darkness.

Even in hard times, find joy in the Lord, who alone is worthy of praise. Though worldly things may disappoint, draw strength from God, the Almighty Savior. Let His light shine through you, so others may follow your example and be led straight to the cross.

January 19

1 Chronicles 28:9

Do you remember being asked as a child if you cleaned your room? Was your response "yes" even though all you did was cram everything into the closet? Your parents most likely already knew the truth when they asked. The same is to be said for God, He knows every thought long before you think it.

How often have you reluctantly volunteered at church or helped a friend simply out of obligation rather than eagerly anticipating the joy of serving? While others may be unaware of our real motivations, God sees our true intentions.

God promises that if we seek Him, we will find Him. To seek God, we must first turn to His word. Then we are called to serve Him joyfully by using the gifts He has given us to expand His Kingdom. He does not want us serving out of obligation, but rather with joy and fulfillment.

When the Lord calls us, we must answer with courage and faith, doing the work He has given us. He commands us to be strong and brave, promising to always be with us. We trust that He who began this good work in us will carry it on to completion, glorifying us so that we may glorify Him.

January 20

Nehemiah 6:16

As we walk on God's path, the devil will try any tactic to lead us astray, including causing distractions to deter us from fulfilling our purpose and using fear to discourage us. He will exploit anyone and anything available to prevent our success.

Though it may feel like everything's going wrong, remember that these trials are not signs of failure. The devil attempts to undermine our faith just as he did in Eden, but we must not surrender to doubt or discouragement. We can persevere by trusting in our Savior.

God will provide everything we need and strengthen our efforts if He calls us to a task. Though the work may be difficult, God has promised blessings for completing it. We need only show up and see it through to the end.

We achieve glory by doing God's work according to His timing and His methods. Every good gift comes from above, including challenges that give us opportunities to overcome difficulties through His strength rather than our own.

When in doubt, stay rooted in God's word, and finish the race by completing the task the Lord has given you.

January 21

Isaiah 54:17

God is a faithful Husband to us, His bride, even when we act unfaithfully. Despite our transgressions, God remains committed to the relationship and repeatedly forgives us, restoring us to righteousness. He defends us against condemnation and lovingly redeems our brokenness.

Our Husband never promised that weapons wouldn't come against us; He simply assured us they would not succeed. We belong to Him, so our enemies are His enemies, and He is never vanquished. Though we may feel defeated at times, our triumph is through Him.

Though the world witnessed Jesus crucified and assumed it was the end, it was only the beginning. What is seen with human eyes can be misleading, for the greatest battle rages unseen in the spiritual realm. Thus, we must fight not by fleshly means but through the Spirit of Jesus dwelling within us.

When life's storms overwhelm us, it's easy to feel forgotten and alone. But just because God seems silent now does not mean He won't act. His promises remain true for all believers. Though circumstances may not be ideal, God sees the full picture. He loves you with an everlasting love and will not abandon you now.

January 22

Matthew 4:19

Jesus, out of His great love for us, invites us to walk in His footsteps. When we respond to His call and receive salvation, we are also called to share His message with others. We are chosen and entrusted with spreading the gospel.

Once we repent and fully surrender ourselves to God, we become transformed into something entirely new. Those around us take notice of these changes and may inquire about what prompted our renewal. We must always be prepared to share our faith when others ask about the source of our transformation.

In an extraordinary act of love and grace, God became human and endured immense suffering in order to offer salvation and eternal life in Heaven to all people. We should step out of our comfort zone and engage with new people so that they have the opportunity to hear the good news and be saved. We may be someone's only connection to learning about Jesus.

By sharing your personal experiences and story of faith, you can provide hope and healing to others facing similar struggles. Your testimony has the power to offer understanding and inspiration.

January 23

Zechariah 4:6

Rather than acting alone, we are designed to be connected to God, like branches attached to a vine. When we remain close to Him, we become more fruitful, though He may prune us at times so that we flourish. Apart from God, our efforts are futile, but joined with Him, we can accomplish great things.

God will always provide us with what we need to fulfill our responsibilities. However, He does desire that we call on Him, and fight our battles by trusting in Him rather than reacting emotionally or impulsively. By trusting in God's almighty power to work through us, we can achieve far more than we could on our own.

When faced with adversity, we may feel tempted to abandon hope or make hasty decisions. Yet the Lord assures us that He will accomplish His purposes according to His wisdom and timing. If something lies outside His will, no amount of money, influence, skill, or means can bring it to pass.

Have faith, the Lord is always at work and will personally guide every endeavor you undertake. If God is on your side, who can stand against you?

Nahum 1:15

Though God has faced opposition throughout history, those who stand against Him ultimately face defeat, whether swiftly or slowly as divine justice unfolds.

We are all God's children; therefore, those who oppose us also oppose Him. Although we face hardships, God can bring deliverance to glorify His name that we bear. As God's children, we can look forward to an eternity of peace, free from sin and temptation, in His presence.

God is the all-powerful judge. When His anger is unleashed, none who face it can get away. However, He can also shield those who have faith in Him. He never has to strike more than once.

Whatever darkness you are facing now, remember God is already working to guide you through. If you take His hand and follow His lead in obedience to His word, He will break the yoke upon you and tear off your shackles.

Jesus promises that anyone who perseveres as He did will share in His authority to rule the Earth. Our God assures us that through Jesus we always triumph. Therefore, rejoice in the victory awaiting you through Christ our Lord!

January 25

2 Corinthians 2:15

According to God's word, those saved by grace possess a sweet fragrance emanating from Christ Himself. As we grow in grace and faith, abiding in God's word and submitting to the Holy Spirit's guidance, we exude an aroma that delights God.

Christ dwells within us and manifests through our lives. We embody His presence in the world by modeling His actions, decisions, and speech. Our mindset contrasts profoundly with those adhering to worldly standards.

Wherever we go and whatever we do, we leave behind the scent of Jesus to encourage others to embrace His ways. Our lives become a living reminder of Christ's goodness, mercy, courage, and love, positively influencing those around us.

The scent of holiness can also repel those dead in their sins, as it makes them more aware of their own sinfulness and need for salvation. When you encounter this type of opposition, do not be discouraged - Jesus faced this opposition too.

Embrace your new identity and calling as an active ambassador of Christ, reflecting His light and leading others to salvation for the glory of God's name.

Judges 18:5

We often embark on our agendas without first seeking God's guidance. It's easy to operate on autopilot, plunging headfirst into pursuing our many goals.

Imagine how many catastrophes we would avoid if we started each day by quietly reflecting in God's presence with a hot cup of coffee and Bible in hand.

To fulfill God's agenda, we must relinquish our own. Our purpose is to carry out His will, not our own desires. The key to discerning if we are on the right track is to first connect with Him and patiently await His response.

It is essential to maintain a network of fellow believers in Christ whom we can reach out to for guidance and support. By having a few trusted brothers and sisters on speed dial, we can ensure that our ideas align with God's path. Their valuable input can assist us in refining our approach and generating helpful ideas.

Being a disciple of Jesus involves understanding effective strategies and recognizing ineffective ones. It is important to remember that God's plans are always designed with our well-being in mind. Once you have discerned His will, follow it obediently, and He will ensure its success.

January 27

2 Samuel 24:24

After we have sincerely repented and abandoned our sinful behaviors, it is imperative that we develop a fervent longing to dedicate ourselves to God and utilize our time, efforts, and possessions in a manner that reflects our commitment to Him. This entails emulating Jesus and embodying the concept of a living sacrifice.

Sacrificing to God necessitates a personal cost. Fortunately, Jesus has already paid the highest price to open the path to Heaven, yet we must willingly surrender our own desires and ambitions to emulate His example. By dedicating ourselves daily, we can truly embody the principles of God's Kingdom.

One way to achieve this is by setting aside our phones, turning off the television, and dedicating quality time to our family and friends.

Additionally, we can reach out to our neighbors and the elderly, provide meals to those who are in need, participate in community service, donate the money intended for shopping to charity, or engage in any act of kindness that requires a sacrifice.

Rely on the Lord when you give, and He will reveal to you the areas where help is needed. You will never need to worry about giving too much, as He will always supply according to His plan.

January 28

Philippians 3:13-14

Have you ever attempted to swim across a lake while lugging a suitcase filled with bricks? I haven't either. However, that's similar to what it feels like when you hold onto the weight of the past instead of releasing it and moving forward in life.

We must not let the setbacks of yesterday hinder us from fulfilling our divine purpose today. It is essential that we master the ability to lick our wounds and persevere. The Almighty is our ultimate source of restoration, and if we grant Him the chance, He will heal every injury we have endured and restore us completely.

Reflecting on the regrets and missed opportunities of the past will only thwart your progress. It's inevitable that as humans, we all go through some kind of significant hardship in our lives. Instead, let's focus on Jesus, who guides us towards perfecting our faith.

All the prizes we pursue in this earthly life are fleeting. The things that belong to God, however, are everlasting. It is crucial for us to practice self-control and listen to the divine calling, as we have an eternal crown of glory awaiting us in Heaven.

January 29

Job 1:7

Pay close attention to the message conveyed in this scripture. It's interesting to note that God already knew Satan's whereabouts, yet He still asked him. Satan's response is quite revealing - he was actively observing and monitoring the happenings on Earth. It's evident that he was scheming and plotting something significant.

Currently, Earth serves as Satan's dwelling place. He and his defiant legion of angels freely wander, exerting their influence to propagate all conceivable and inconceivable forms of wickedness, utilizing any means and individuals at their disposal.

Please take note that Satan was limited to bringing his complaints and accusations to God, unable to act independently of God's will. Satan had to seek permission beforehand, which serves as evidence that God maintains ultimate authority even over the devil. It is a testament that nothing occurs without God's allowance.

Satan is always trying to make you question God's goodness. Even though we may not understand why we face certain trials, we can be sure that those who hold onto their faith will come out victorious.

January 30

Psalms 46:10

If you share a similar disposition as mine, I have a drive to actively engage and manage every circumstance, aiming to steer it towards my desired outcome. The notion of sitting back and unwinding is not a phrase that frequently appears in my daily personal dictionary.

It is God's will for us to release control, embracing our vulnerability as we depend on His sustenance and strength. Paradoxically, our strength is revealed in our weakness. This truth can be particularly challenging when we have tried every possible solution and find ourselves confronted with what appears to be a hopeless situation.

How can we find peace and calm amidst the chaos of life's storms? One way is to turn to God and express our needs and gratitude for guiding us through every storm we've faced. Instead of constantly pushing and struggling, we should find solace in His presence and patiently await His answer.

There is no need to be afraid when we have the Almighty Creator on our side. Set aside a moment of silence to reflect on the wonders of God in your personal journey. Be still and marvel at all He has done this far.

January 31

Proverbs 28:13

There are three options available when dealing with sin: rejecting it, concealing it, or admitting to it. It can be challenging to forgive individuals who evade taking responsibility for their mistakes, opting instead to make excuses and shift blame.

God assures us that all evil actions done in secret will eventually be exposed. The Lord declares that if we openly admit our wrongdoings, He is compassionate and ready to pardon us, erasing our transgressions completely. Moreover, not only does He offer forgiveness, but He also showers us with blessings through His boundless mercy.

Forgiving someone and showing grace becomes simpler when they humbly acknowledge their mistake and change their ways. By choosing not to confess our sins to each other, we miss out on potential blessings.

This also applies when we confront ourselves. We may attempt to deceive ourselves and rationalize our wrongdoing, but the Holy Spirit will make us aware when we deviate from God's plan. Any sin we try to conceal will eventually come to light. However, it's our response to it that determines our fate.

February

Isaiah 2:17

Have you ever heard someone talk proudly about achieving success solely through their own hard work, without any assistance from others? They often boast about it, only to later experience a humbling event such as illness, financial loss, or personal tragedy.

Losing awareness of God's presence in our lives can lead to pride and the worship of false idols. Instead of bragging about ourselves, we should proudly acknowledge the Lord as the source of all good things, regardless of our own contributions.

It is clear that God does not approve of pride, as demonstrated by the consequences that the devil faced. Being blessed and chosen does not give us the right to view ourselves as better than others. Our actions reflect the true nature of our hearts. If we fail to humble ourselves, the Lord will humble us in front of numerous witnesses.

Developing personal growth involves recognizing both our strengths and weaknesses without being prideful or insecure. Jesus taught us that humility leads to greatness, so we should strive to live humbly like Him. Jesus was confident in His identity and abilities, setting an example for us to emulate.

February 2

Ecclesiastes 3:1

If we had things our way, we'd get what we desire whenever we desire it. Can you picture a world where everyone always got what they wanted? It would be utter chaos with each person having their own vision of how things should be.

There is an appointed time for everything, yet it may not always align with our own schedule. Our compassionate God consistently bestows His grace upon us, guiding us towards His flawless resolution at the perfect moment. By placing our trust in Him, we will discover that His ways surpass our own in every aspect.

It can be disheartening as we navigate through life, making decisions we believe are faithful, only to end up waiting ceaselessly for our dreams to come true. Sometimes, things don't go as planned at all. All we can do is have faith, be patient, remain hopeful, and witness the Lord revealing His plan in His own timing.

It is true that we may not fully comprehend the entirety of God's work from start to finish. However, this journey can be both challenging and awe-inspiring, as it molds our faith and deepens our connection with Him. It enables us to examine our intentions and align our aspirations with His divine purpose.

February 3

Lamentations 3:32

Following the passing of my younger brother, the agony of his absence became too much to bear. I experienced a continuous cycle of grief, struggling to cope with the overwhelming emotions. There were days when simply getting out of bed seemed like an impossible task.

My attention was consumed by my own pain and his untimely departure, causing me to overlook the peace that could have been found in turning to Jesus beyond my anger.

After I stopped blaming God and acknowledged the reality of the situation, I recognized that my actions were only causing me more pain. I humbly approached God, laying down all my grievances and concerns, seeking a peace beyond what I could comprehend.

Afterwards, I couldn't help but express my gratitude to God for the precious moments I had with my brother and the joyful memories we created together. It was a turning point in my healing process, as it reminded me that I am not the one in charge and that the people I cherish are merely temporary blessings from God.

Our compassionate Father eagerly awaits to provide comfort and nurture our growth amidst our sorrows.

February 4

Ezekiel 36:9

As Spring approaches, I absolutely adore living in the Midwest. It's incredible to witness the once barren land burst into a kaleidoscope of vibrant colors. The sweet aroma of farmers burning their land to prepare the soil for planting fills the air, creating a warm and comforting atmosphere.

It's like a gentle nudge that awakens my senses, reminding me of the beauty and signs of life that surround us. This experience never fails to evoke a sense of nostalgic comfort within me. Emerging from tough times and going through God's purification process is quite similar to this.

Every stroke of God's plow is tilling the ground of your heart in anticipation of receiving the seed of His word, which is none other than Jesus Christ Himself. He is diligently nourishing your soul with the presence of His one and only son.

We were made to be fruitful. When we recognize Jesus as our source, we start to produce amazing things for His Kingdom in a supernatural way. Our lives reflect God's character, showing that we are genuinely His children.

Cultivating and planting isn't always easy, but it will yield a plentiful crop. It's important to nurture the soil in our hearts with the teachings of God.

February 5

Daniel 3:25

We can find solace in knowing that no matter how intense the challenges we face may be, we are never alone as the Lord is by our side. Despite the daunting appearance of these trials, God will guide us safely through them. By holding onto this belief, we can seek comfort and remain unwavering in our faith as we follow His divine plan.

It is possible to feel as though we have been forsaken by God or that our pleas for compassion have gone unheard, however, this is simply not the case. We were never promised an easy journey. We are called to share in both the hardships and the victories of Jesus.

Indeed, our resilience is unparalleled, enabling us to endure infernos that would prove fatal to most. Nebuchadnezzar, symbolizing the world, commands the flames to intensify sevenfold, resulting in the demise of the soldiers who epitomize those adhering to worldly norms just by approaching it.

Nevertheless, we are under the protection of God. We might need to defend our faith against a multitude and even walk through fire, but we are confident that not a single hair on our heads will be harmed unless it is in accordance with God's plan.

February 6

Matthew 7:3

We all tend to pass judgment on others without taking a moment to reflect on ourselves. It is common for us to believe that resolving issues would be simpler if the other person altered their behavior, all the while disregarding the blatant hypocrisy that is evident to everyone around us.

That doesn't imply that the individual in question is faultless, it just suggests that our attention should be on the improvements we must make.

After eliminating the source of sin from our own lives, our vision will become clearer. Once we have resolved this matter, we will be able to assist others in a more loving manner to remove the small flaw from their eye.

The purpose of this passage is to emphasize the importance of setting aside pride in order to compassionately assist our fellow believers in Christ. It highlights the significance of our attitude when addressing the wrongdoing of others.

It is important to always keep in mind our dependence on God's grace, as this enables us to share it with those around us.

February 7

Malachi 4:2

The Almighty has forewarned us that the day of reckoning is approaching. It's bound to happen, there's no escaping it. Each and every one of us will be held accountable by Him. However, this passage brings solace to those who hold His name in high regard.

Those of us who have faith are assured that when the day of judgment comes, our merciful God will forgive us, safeguard us, heal us, and show us mercy. Furthermore, He will empower us to trample over the wicked as easily as dust beneath our feet.

Just like the sun symbolizes Jesus, it brings life to each new day, providing warmth and radiating immense power. There is no reason for us to be afraid, as there is no condemnation for those who have a relationship with Christ Jesus.

The passage also describes a happy scene of what God has planned for us, likening us to playful calves frolicking in an open field. It's a day we should eagerly anticipate, free from the negativity the world often presents.

We are fortunate to have the opportunity to seek forgiveness before the dawn of righteousness. Let us assist those around us in doing the same before it is too late.

February 8

Micah 6:8

I've lost count of how many times I've asked God, "What do you want me to do?" There are numerous days when I feel overwhelmed or uncertain, wondering if I'm heading in the right direction. The answer to this lingering question can be found in this scripture.

What does it signify to act in accordance with righteousness, embrace compassion, and lead a humble life in the presence of God? God has revealed to us the path of righteousness and goodness by sending Jesus Christ as an example.

Acting justly entails adhering to moral principles, while mercy is demonstrated through the love and grace we show towards others. Walking humbly requires us to be conscious of our actions and how they align with our beliefs.

All aspects have been streamlined here, yet it covers His divine expectations entirely. Our aim is to live in a manner that mirrors Him more and ourselves less, aligning our thoughts with the compassionate heart of Jesus.

By following these strategies designated for life, we can experience our fullest potential, receive abundant blessings, and bring joy to others, ultimately pleasing our Heavenly Father.

February 9

Psalms 13:1

This passage always reminds me of the time when the Israelites roamed the desert for 40 years in pursuit of the Promised Land. God assured them of a blessed destination at the end of their journey, but He never guaranteed a swift or easy journey. All He asked for was their faith.

Our journey through life is no different. We are assured of a Heavenly destination that will last for eternity, as long as we embrace our Savior and stay faithful as we navigate the path towards our eternal Promised Land.

I can only fathom the multitude of prayers that were lifted up to the Lord, pleading, "How much longer? How far must we still travel before this comes to an end?" During times of ease, it is simple to sense God's presence, but when challenges arise, it is natural to wonder what actions have caused God to seemingly ignore our pleas.

When you feel like God isn't answering your prayers, try to find joy in your salvation, even in the toughest times. Have faith in His mercy and trust that He will provide for you. Remember to be grateful for all the blessings He has given you. Just keep believing, He will guide you through, as He always does.

February 10

Proverbs 1:10

As humans, we will always encounter temptation, but there's a distinction between dealing with our own temptations and succumbing to the temptations others present to us. The age-old saying, "Misery loves company," holds undeniable truth.

The individuals we choose to have in our lives play a significant role in determining our achievements and setbacks. It is clearly mentioned in the scriptures that associating with negative influences can lead to the deterioration of our values.

Even with good intentions, if we associate with those heading down a harmful road, we may end up facing the same consequences. Jesus, who faced temptation from the devil three times, remained steadfast in His identity and in God's word, causing the devil to flee.

We should emulate Jesus' example when confronted with tempting pressures from those around us. It is imperative to have a strong foundation in God's word so that even if someone distorts it, we can discern its true meaning. The devil will try to tempt us repeatedly when we are at our most vulnerable. However, if we resist the devil, he will eventually flee from us.

February 11

Psalms 30:11

Once Jesus rescued me and I began embarking on my new journey in life, I started grieving for certain aspects of my previous life. Despite God's efforts to gather all the shattered fragments and mend them, I still felt a pang of sadness for what had been left behind.

As I contemplated the dark moments in my life, I came to the realization that I was living under God's judgement due to my sinful ways. Despite His disapproval of my actions, God intervened to guide me towards a better path.

Though His interventions may have been tough, His love for me was evident as He desired a brighter future for me - a future for which He sacrificed His only son, Jesus Christ. I felt a profound sense of peace in my heart as I acknowledged the grace that was given to me in guiding me back home.

The pivotal moment in my life was when I encountered the cross. God transformed every obstacle meant to harm me into a testimony that magnified His name and reign. He rescued me from despair, and now I delight in Him by embracing a journey of renewal, healing, and trust. His presence ignites a fire within me, changing my mourning into dancing.

February 12

1 Peter 2:9

Have you ever got out of bed in the morning, walked over to the mirror, and looked at your reflection while saying, "I am chosen, I am royalty, I am Holy! My Father is the Almighty, and nothing can stand in my way as I follow His divine plan!"

If you haven't given it a shot yet, now is the perfect time to do so, because that's exactly who you are!

It is essential to remember your worth and remind yourself of your value in a world that will attempt to diminish it. Make it a daily practice to acknowledge who you are and how special you truly are!

The significance of all this is clear: you possess authority. You are able to advocate for others, approach the throne of God as your Father, and thwart every attack from the devil.

Living a life of holiness is not inherent to human nature. Those who lead holy lives do so through the grace of God, and by making a conscious daily decision to walk in a dignified manner that reflects our royal identity.

We are like a ripple effect in the water, our actions echoing through generations. Choose wisely, for we are a reflection of the Lord's resonance.

February 13

Isaiah 8:12

There are countless things in our surroundings that could potentially make us live in fear on a daily basis. We might worry about a car accident whenever we're on the road, fear for our safety in crowded places, or be concerned about skin cancer from sun exposure.

The way in which we experience fear, and the object of our fear reveals who we fear. Our devotion should be directed towards fearing God. We are not instructed to fear the same things that unbelievers fear.

To fear God is to show respect, have faith, and hold Him in high esteem. If we have reverence for our Lord, we understand that there is no reason to be afraid in this worldly existence, as perfect love eradicates all forms of fear.

No matter what darkness may await us, we can take comfort in the fact that Jesus has already gone ahead of us and faced it head-on. As we navigate through life, we will undoubtedly encounter obstacles, but we need not fear any future darkness because our Lord will always be there, guiding us with the light of His grace.

February 14

Hosea 2:23

In the same way Hosea extended grace to his wife, God showers us with grace, loving us unconditionally despite our sins. If you've been avoiding God, remember that nothing can sever His love for you. He always longs for us, the choice to return home to Him is ours alone.

We, the chosen ones, are likened to seeds sown by God. We are the select seeds, carefully separated from the others, destined to grow into a harvest fit for the Almighty Himself.

The Bible is a beautiful love story, brimming with flawless affection right from the start. It then transforms into a narrative of an unfaithful wife, shedding light on the challenges she faced, and the difficulties endured by her faithful and loving Husband in His pursuit to reclaim her.

Ultimately, thc wife, with humility and gratitude, reunites with her Husband, leading to a blissful and everlasting life together. There is no greater love story than this.

This isn't just a love story, it's your story! You can proudly declare the name of your loving Husband - the name you gracefully bear for all to know.

Obadiah 1:12

It's natural for us to experience a feeling of contentment when we see someone who we believe has treated us unfairly face the consequences of their actions. However, God wants us, His children, to show compassion towards others, just as He has shown us compassion.

If we exhibit a malicious nature and find pleasure in the misfortunes of others, regardless of how evil or unkind they may be, it indicates that our hearts have indeed remained unchanged. God has made a promise to transform our stony hearts into tender and empathetic hearts of flesh.

When we are born again, we are selected to lead selfless lives, always mindful of how our decisions and actions affect those around us. Pride is detested by God. We must not simply watch and revel in the suffering of others. God will judge all our deeds, even the ones we keep hidden.

The grace of the Lord is meant to lead us away from sin, and our acts of kindness in an unkind world could potentially lead even an enemy to turn away from their wickedness towards repentance and salvation in Jesus Christ. Allow God's light to shine through you and touch the lives of those around you today.

February 16

Mark 16:15

I'm not sure about you, but I absolutely adore hearing good news! It brings me so much joy when my loved ones reach out to share the blessings in their lives, allowing me to celebrate alongside them.

Often, this good news is the result of enduring hardships and waiting patiently, which makes it even more special and fills my heart with gratitude for the blessings of God in their lives.

I always make it a point to thank God whenever I hear good news, recognizing that all good things come from Him. Jesus Christ is the ultimate good news from our Father in Heaven, and sharing this good news literally breathes life into all who receive it.

There are countless blessings in our lives that we often overlook, like having clean water, access to food, the ability to read, hearing our favorite music, feeling the warmth of the sun, the companionship of a beloved pet, and most importantly, our redemption.

Let's remember to thank God for His blessings and spread love and hope wherever we go, so that others can experience the joy of Jesus Christ.

February 17

Romans 8:29

God reveals in this touching passage that He had foreknowledge of those who would choose to follow Him even before their birth. He had a clear understanding of those who would willingly embrace the character of Jesus Christ through grace, and strive to become more like Him.

The love of God towards us originated in eternity and will forever reside there. We have been embraced into a royal family by a compassionate Father overflowing with grace, alongside a remarkable older brother who serves as a role model. This brother conquered challenges that would seem insurmountable to us without His guidance.

We should be willing to endure suffering as Jesus did, in order to be obedient to our Heavenly Father. By following in the footsteps of our elder brother, we can be assured that we will attain glory, just as He did. God had a specific purpose for Jesus, and He has also assigned a unique purpose for each one of us.

We should always remember that we are never alone in our sorrows or our joy. We belong to the biggest, most caring family ever formed. Even if we didn't grow up in the same home, our Father brings us together to show love and provide support for each other.

Galatians 5:22-24

When we transition from darkness to light, it is important for that light to shine through us wherever we go. Our attitudes and beliefs should be visible to everyone. We should be consistent in our stance, so that those around us can always rely on us.

Before the fruits of the Spirit can be visible in our lives, we need to remove the weeds of sin with the guidance of Jesus Christ. These fruits start to show more prominently not through our own actions, but by conforming to the teachings of God.

It's not easy for us to embrace these fruits, as they go against our natural instincts. Developing qualities like patience and self-control can be tough, but the more you work on removing selfishness, the more you'll see the positive impact of the fruits of the Spirit in your life.

Denying our worldly desires by nailing them to the cross of Jesus is not imposed upon us, but rather a decision we actively make. This is a daily commitment we must uphold. It is not enough to simply carry our cross and walk in the footsteps of Jesus; we must ensure that our sinful tendencies are put to death, crucified on the cross.

February 19

Ephesians 4:31

We may not have control over how our rude co-worker or disgruntled neighbor treats us, but we have the power to respond to them with kindness regardless of their behavior.

There have been occasions when I experienced my temper rising during discussions with non-believers and fellow Christians. It can be challenging to resist the urge to react impulsively and instead choose to respond with the love and grace of Jesus.

Each trait discussed in this passage can be compared to a form of soul cancer slowly consuming you. The damage it inflicts on you is ultimately more harmful than the wound it inflicted on the receiving party.

Jesus exhibited a form of justified anger when he overturned the tables at the temple, however, this passage addresses habitual anger stemming from frequent irritations. It encourages us to rid ourselves of this anger and embody the characteristics of Christ instead.

We come across many people every day, but the only person we genuinely have power over is ourselves. Forgiveness is possible because we have been forgiven. With the help of God's grace, we can learn to let go and let God.

February 20

Exodus 20:12

Family serves as the basis of our lives. Every connection we form originates within the walls of our home. It is evident that family holds utmost importance, as emphasized by our divine Creator. This is the very essence of what God has established and continues to nurture.

By honoring our mothers and fathers, God promises us a longer life and abundant blessings in the land. This principle remains relevant today as we appreciate the valuable lessons we learn from our parents' examples.

Our parents play a pivotal role in our lives as our first encounter with figures of authority. They play a crucial part in instilling in us the values, behaviors, and attitudes necessary for our growth and development. They shape the moral compass that guides us throughout our lives.

Respecting our parents should not be contingent upon their treatment towards us or the material possessions they offer. It is an act of reverence that transcends external factors. Love can serve as a compass, guiding us towards the most meaningful ways to demonstrate honor.

February 21

Genesis 4:7

This passage portrays sin as a persistent presence, patiently waiting outside your door, eagerly anticipating your surrender. However, the key takeaway here is that we possess the ability to conquer it!

Given this understanding, it is imperative that we opt for a life of mindfulness rather than succumbing to fear. Sin possesses a cunning and deceitful nature. It has the ability to exploit our noble intentions, and if we are not vigilant, it can subtly distort things to the point where you may start doubting God's authority completely.

Sin is an act of defiance, and if left unchecked, it can ultimately result in death. When we recognize our sins, the most effective course of action is to distance ourselves from them, seek solace in prayer, and reach out to fellow believers for support.

Make sure to put a strategic plan into action and maintain it consistently. By focusing on conquering one weakness at a time, you'll find it easier to protect yourself from other temptations lurking nearby. Remember to immerse yourself in God's word every day and equip yourself with His armor each morning, so that you can triumph with the help of Jesus Christ, our Lord!

February 22

Job 16:20

Job made the faithful decision to express his heartfelt prayers to God and stayed strong in his belief, ignoring the judgments of others, and confronting each hardship with a humble awareness of the identity of his intercessor long before His arrival as Jesus Christ.

In this journey of life, every challenge we encounter is merely a fleeting moment when compared to the everlasting joy that awaits us. However, during this time, our savior is always there, tirelessly advocating for us and bringing us closer to our Father.

If we are to emulate the path of Jesus, it is imperative that we also engage in intercession on behalf of others. We should fervently lift up prayers to God, earnestly pleading for His intervention in the midst of any hardships they may be facing.

This passage exemplifies the potency of prayer presented to our merciful Father. He is eager to listen to our pleas. Intercession possesses great power, capable of averting God's anger and receiving His blessings instead.

When you pray to Jesus for help today, remember to also pray for someone else and be the kind of friend to them that Jesus is to you.

February 23

Psalms 23:5

Jesus serves as a Shepherd to us, ensuring our safety and guarding us from harm. While there may be those who wish to see us fail, our loving Shepherd guides us with care and protection.

Our Heavenly Host, filled with grace, has prepared the table before us in the presence of all those surrounding us. We acknowledge our dependence on Him and have faith that all our needs will be fulfilled through His grace. He has never disappointed us, and He never will.

I'd like to mention something else. While we relish the blessings bestowed upon us by the Lord, we must also acknowledge that our adversaries are observing us closely. Rather than boasting about our blessings, why not take this chance to extend an invitation to them and welcome them to join us at the table?

We used to be enemies of God, lost in sin. Thanks to Jesus inviting us to His table, we were saved from starvation. As part of God's family, it's our responsibility to welcome others and offer them a seat. The choice to accept the invitation is theirs to make.

Our cups overflow, may we relish in our abundance and generously give to others in a manner that honors God.

February 24

Proverbs 2:11

Those who possess wisdom have the ability to anticipate and plan ahead, making connections that others may not see. By understanding, you can predict the consequences of the decisions you are about to make.

God has bestowed upon us a divine roadmap to navigate through this journey called life, through His sacred scriptures and the exemplary life of Jesus Christ. These invaluable resources serve as a shield, guarding us against a life plagued with anguish, turmoil, and hardship.

Within them lies the secret to victory and prosperity. By prioritizing our relationship with God, we unlock a whole new lens through which we perceive the world, transforming our perspective in the most remarkable ways.

Trust your instincts and listen to the gentle nudges of the Holy Spirit within your conscience. It is a divine signal, a message from God Himself, guiding you towards a new path. Embrace it with open arms and allow yourself to be redirected towards a greater purpose.

February 25

Joel 2:25

The devastation caused by Locusts invading a crop is extensive, as they not only consume the current crop and the seed from the previous year, but also the seed required for planting next year's crop. Recovering from such destruction takes years and new seeds are needed.

This passage serves as a reflection of God's righteous judgment and His pledge to renew everything that was taken away from those who seek forgiveness, providing a glimmer of hope for blessings and renewal.

Our compassionate Father never fails to offer His hand filled with grace and mercy, even when we become too comfortable with His blessings. Through challenges, He gently nudges us to rekindle our connection with Him, like a skilled gardener carefully pruning his plants.

He carried the weight of our sins, confronted judgment, and endured immense suffering on the cross. He willingly took on our burdens and sacrificed Himself to open a path towards eternal glory for us.

He extends His hand, assuring us that He will restore all that hardships have taken away, but it is our choice to grasp it.

February 26

Zephaniah 3:17

God's presence in our lives is unwavering, and His love knows no bounds. His affection and attention towards us are beyond measure. Remember, God is not only present in your life, but He also finds immense joy in your very existence!

Your Father's perception of you is seen through the lens of Jesus' sacrifice and the redemption achieved at the cross. Every aspect of your sin has been fully atoned for. The sole significance lies in leading a life completely devoted to God. A life surrendered to God, earnestly seeking His presence, brings immense joy to Him.

It's time to rejoice, not because everything is going perfectly according to our desires, but because we have a compassionate Father who embraces us with open arms, overjoyed to have us back in His presence. Our mistakes and failures are forever out of sight.

Choose to celebrate today with your Heavenly Father and bask in His presence in your life. Let Him transform your sadness into joy, and craft something lovely from your struggles. Rush into His warm embrace and find serenity there.

February 27

Matthew 17:20

God has blessed us with life, love, and abundance without asking for much in return. All He desires is a small amount of faith from us. He respects our free will and will never impose His will upon us. It is up to us to choose whether to have faith in Him or to go our own way.

The mustard seed is a powerful symbol of the incredible impact that a small amount of faith can make. Despite its tiny size, when sown in fertile soil, it has the ability to grow into a magnificent plant, defying all odds even in the harshest of conditions.

Jesus never mentioned that the mountain would instantly move; He simply stated that it could be moved with even a small amount of faith. Similar to how a plant takes time to grow, our faith may also require some time to develop and eventually move the mountain.

Seeds possess an unwavering determination, refusing to surrender as they crack open and persevere through the depths of the soil, reaching for the radiant embrace of sunlight. Just like the small mustard seed, we can overcome any obstacle with a little amount of faith.

John 17:3

In essence, there are two kinds of people: those who have embraced Jesus Christ as their Savior, and those who have not. So, what does it signify to have Jesus as your Savior? It signifies that Salvation is not earned through our efforts, but through acknowledging the selfless act He carried out on the cross.

In the Bible, the concept of "knowing" holds a profound significance. It involves establishing a deep connection with another person, a shared indwelling. Therefore, to "know" God is to understand every personal, intimate detail about Him - His preferences, His boundaries, His emotions, and beyond.

To experience salvation and attain eternal life, it is essential to develop a personal relationship with God through Jesus Christ. By accepting Jesus as your Savior and emulating His teachings, you can embark on a path towards everlasting peace.

Remember, the only way to reach the Father is through His son, Jesus. He serves as the bridge connecting our earthly life to the eternal happiness of Heaven. Once you accept Jesus as your savior, you can be confident that the wonderful gift of Heaven is right at your fingertips.

February 29

Acts 11:14

Can you imagine what your life would look like if you had never come to know Jesus and be saved? It's incredible to think that it all started because someone took the time to tell you about Him and how to find salvation.

God's divine plan unfolded when He chose to send Jesus to Earth. His intention was to ensure that the message of salvation reached every corner of the world, granting everyone the chance to experience the love of their Creator.

The Bible has the amazing ability to transform our hearts and impact our lives, much like it did in the story of Genesis. With just a word from God, everything was created. This powerful book has the ability to breathe life into our world and perform miracles in our daily lives.

Jesus Christ came into this world like a seed planted as a vine, and we are His branches meant to reach out to others and share the message of salvation through Him. It is our responsibility as believers to step out of our comfort zones and lead people back to their Heavenly home.

By following His lead and seizing the opportunities He provides, we can trust that He will handle the rest - all we need to do is be present and willing to do our part.

March

March 1

Romans 8:37

You are an unstoppable force! You have emerged victorious in every challenge you have encountered, and you will continue to do so because Jesus is your guiding light.

The indomitable power that resides within you is invincible! No matter where life takes you or what obstacles come your way, you possess all the strength and resilience needed to overcome them.

At times, achieving victory can be as simple as getting out of bed in the morning and confronting the day, while on other occasions, it entails having courage and finding solace in the Lord while grappling with a life-threatening illness. The realm of victory encompasses many diverse forms.

This assurance doesn't guarantee victory in the world's eyes. We will undoubtedly encounter challenges, difficulties, and even mortality, but it is our response to these circumstances that showcases our unwavering faith in God. He is constantly orchestrating everything for our benefit, and nothing can ever sever us from His boundless love.

Trusting in God's promises enables us to break free from the grip of our circumstances, leading us to discover the true source of our victory.

March 2

1 Corinthians 15:33

It's pretty common to have had a friend or two that our parents didn't exactly love. Sometimes we only see the truth in their warnings when something goes wrong. The people we surround ourselves with say a lot about who we are.

Community is a conscious decision we make, where we can either opt to embrace the company of fellow believers in Christ or choose otherwise. Our path can only lead us in two directions: drawing nearer to Him or drifting farther away.

According to the Bible, just as iron sharpens iron, spending time with fellow believers who share our enthusiasm for Jesus can greatly strengthen our connection with Him. On the other hand, if we choose differently, our lives will inevitably reflect that decision.

It's wise to take an honest inventory of the relationships we choose to keep in our lives. We need to ask ourselves if they are helping us grow in our relationship to God, or if they are obstructing our view of Him.

It is also important for us to reflect on our own actions and consider whether we are setting an example as faithful friends guiding others towards spiritual growth.

March 3

Romans 12:1

After receiving the call to serve, the next task is to discover how we can be of service. To achieve this, we must assess the needs around us and determine how we can contribute based on our unique talents. Understanding our purpose in the church can be a fascinating journey of discovery.

When we offer our service, we are offering ourselves as living sacrifices. This act of worship brings immense joy to our Heavenly Father. To serve in a manner that pleases God, we must actively engage with a willing heart, placing our faith in the Holy Spirit to guide us and equip us with everything required to serve.

It can be incredibly tough at first, but don't give up. Surrendering is never simple, but the more we dedicate ourselves to serving others, the easier it will become. Being a source of positivity and kindness is a gift in itself. There's no greater joy in this world than knowing you've made a difference.

When we anchor our hearts in Jesus, the fruits it produces are limitless and abundant. It becomes a nurturing garden that we share with others, bringing healing and joy. Our physical bodies serve the purpose of showcasing God's grace and glory through the way we live our lives.

March 4

Isaiah 31:1

The foundation of the world is delicate and fractured, constructed upon a flawed structure of money, lust, greed, and power. Eventually, these elements will crumble.

God, however, stands as an everlasting and invincible foundation, separate from any external influences. Every day, we have the privilege to decide which side of the fence we wish to stand on.

In a world that constantly urges us to chase after wealth, independence, and material possessions, it is key to remember the wisdom of God's teachings. He encourages us to place our trust in Him, to embrace humility, and to appreciate the blessings we already have.

By seeking solace in worship and prayer, we can find fulfillment in both our needs and desires. While the world operates within the constraints of time, God's divine presence transcends the boundaries of eternity.

The ways of the Lord are always righteous. Seek His guidance, strength, and wisdom, and you will never be led astray. Practice patience and praise Him while you wait, and you will experience a peace that surpasses worldly understanding.

March 5

James 4:7-8

During Jesus' time in the desert, the devil approached Him with the intention of tempting Him into committing sin. Jesus had been fasting and His hunger was evident. The devil patiently waited, hoping that Jesus would succumb to the temptation once His strength waned.

However, despite His hunger and the allure of Satan's scheme, Jesus bravely resisted three times by using the word of God. Eventually, the devil retreated, leaving Jesus victorious in His battle against temptation.

The devil doesn't force us into sinning; instead, he sows the seeds and presents sin in an appealing manner. Sin, ultimately, is a decision we consciously make, and each decision we make reflects our understanding and connection with God.

The devil tends to strike when we've already faced a string of exhausting events, leaving us barely holding on. So, don't be shocked when that final blow hits, making you feel like you can't endure anymore.

This is when you must hold tight to God's word and promises. Stand firm against the devil's lies, trusting that your caring Father will always be by your side.

March 6

1 Kings 2:2-3

As representatives of God, it's important for us to recognize that this places us in a position of influence. Others will observe our actions, listen to our words, and analyze every aspect of our lives. Therefore, it is of utmost importance that we live in accordance with God's teachings.

We must show strength and bravery by standing up and speaking out when others hesitate. This might make us a target for the devil's attacks, but we can take comfort in knowing that he has already been defeated.

It is important for God's children to obey His word in order to guide others to Jesus. By doing this, our loving Father assures us that we will find success in all our endeavors, even though challenges may arise along the way. Obedience is key.

We have been summoned by God to occupy the most esteemed role bestowed upon humanity. Understanding God's desires and aligning ourselves with His will is imperative, as it is through His will that we receive His abundant blessings.

His grace knows no limits, and we are entrusted with the task of spreading God's will and passing the torch to the generations to come.

March 7

1 Samuel 16:7

I have a vivid memory of my dad taking me shopping for clothes one day. He had just finished his work, and his clothes were full of holes and covered in dirt and sheetrock dust.

Usually, when people walk into a store, they are greeted by a sales associate. However, on that day, we received a few curious glances, but no one came forward to offer us any assistance.

The sales associates had no idea that my dad owned his own construction company and could have easily bought me a whole new wardrobe. They underestimated us based on his appearance, assuming we couldn’t afford much and weren't worth their time.

Praise the Lord for looking beyond our outward appearance, recognizing the true essence of who we are. He sees into our hearts, acknowledging the goodness within us which is a reflection of His love deeply embedded into the very fiber of our being.

The sales associates were on the verge of losing a substantial commission. We could have left the store and taken our business elsewhere. However, their attitudes changed as they were ringing up our purchase. Don’t miss out on potential blessings by prematurely judging others.

Psalms 3:5

As I opened my eyes this morning, I made my way to the living room where I found my husband savoring a cup of coffee while our little dog kept him company. My hair was a mess, and my pajamas were wrinkled, but when my husband looked at me, he smiled warmly and invited me to come cuddle with him.

I had to pause for a moment as overwhelming gratitude filled my heart for the countless blessings surrounding me. God protected me as I slept, allowing me to wake up to this precious moment that moved me to tears of thankfulness.

I was grateful to God for the peaceful night's rest, my kind husband, the dirty dishes that led to a satisfying meal, the laundry waiting to be folded as a reminder of having clothes to wear, the working utilities in our cozy home that we own, and most importantly, I thanked God for His presence and boundless love and grace.

I then expressed my gratitude to God for each and every moment that had brought me to that point, acknowledging my tendency to take such things for granted. I am humbled by the countless times the Lord has protected me from harm, allowing me to wake up each day and acknowledge His blessings and presence.

March 9

Jeremiah 1:8

While I was in prison one morning, I was in the bathroom preparing to brush my teeth when I overheard two young women harassing another woman. They had been tormenting her for weeks due to the odor she carried after working with horses during her work release.

As I witnessed this timid woman enduring numerous struggles, something inside me suddenly snapped. Without hesitation, I decided to confront the two young bullies.

Although fear crept in, knowing we were off camera and I was vulnerable to the possibility of getting jumped, an unstoppable force rose up within me - the mighty roar of the Holy Spirit.

Many women witnessed the ongoing bullying for weeks, too scared to speak out for fear of becoming targets themselves. The dorm was filled with fear, but it seemed that God intervened and selected me to help end it.

I can't recall the exact words I said, but I do remember the two bullies leaving the bathroom together and never bullying her or anyone else again. We can have faith that if God has chosen us to confront a challenge, He will guide us through safely.

Matthew 6:34

I believe this passage is well-known among believers, yet it may be one of the most challenging to live out. It can be tough to avoid worrying about today's problems spilling over into tomorrow, or fretting about what new challenges tomorrow may bring.

Tomorrow holds both uncertainty and hope, as we are unable to predict what lies ahead. It serves as a gentle reminder that we should have faith in God's plan and trust in His guidance.

It is crucial to be mindful of where your focus lies. If you concentrate on fear and uncertainty, these elements will flourish and deprive you of the happiness of the present moment.

By placing your trust in the Lord's promises, guidance, and provision, you can be assured that He will orchestrate everything for your benefit, ensuring that none of your needs go unfulfilled.

No matter how meticulously we plan our lives, if it doesn't align with God's plan, it will all be in vain. Just as God provided manna to the Israelites in the desert every morning, ensuring they had enough food for the day, you can trust that He will take care of you too. By keeping your focus on Him, the burdens of today and the anxieties of tomorrow will fade away.

March 11

John 5:19

When I was young, my mother worked as a hairdresser. I recall accompanying her to work, observing how she interacted with her clients as if they were family.

Her clients would open up to her, sharing their life stories, and upon leaving, they felt a sense of relief from unburdening themselves and a boost in confidence from looking and feeling beautiful after their hair appointments.

As I got older, she started letting me assist with shampooing her clients. I would experiment with different hairstyles on my Barbie dolls and later on my friends. By the age of 18, I had mastered cutting, highlighting, coloring, and styling hair - all without any formal education.

Children possess an extraordinary capacity to absorb everything around them. Their encounters mold their identities. The words they listen to shape the words they speak. They resemble empty canvases, only aware of what they have been taught.

After completing Cosmetology School, I owned two salons and established a salon family of my own. With the knowledge of Christ's love, let us endeavor to love others in the same way He has loved us.

March 12

2 Chronicles 15:7

Have you ever experienced that heart-pounding moment when you were given a promotion or handed a challenging task at work, and a wave of fear washed over you?

Did you find yourself faced with a daunting responsibility that seemed like a mountain too high to climb? I believe we've all encountered this relatable situation at some point in our lives.

Fear is frequently our instinctive reaction. Maintaining strength and courage typically requires consistent reminders and practice, as it can be a continuous effort all on its own.

We each have our own set of tasks to accomplish. While some may be more pleasant than others, by relying on God's strength and trusting in Him, not only will we finish the work, but we can also look forward to the rewards He has promised us.

True bravery is not the lack of fear, but rather the act of trusting in God even in the face of fear. By doing so, we not only affirm our identity in Christ, but also bring glory to God and contribute to the expansion of His Kingdom on Earth, guiding others towards salvation. This act within itself is a reward of its own.

March 13

Psalms 9:12

God listens to every plea and understands your pain. At times, it may seem like our suffering will never end, but our Almighty God has assured us that He will fight for us against those who wrong us when we walk in righteousness.

Our final recourse is not seeking vengeance, but trusting in God's justice. He will bring about justice in due time.

In the same way that God listened to the pleas of His people during their enslavement in Egypt, He has also heard your cries. He devised a master plan to free them, a plan that required years of effort but ultimately triumphed.

Our Heavenly Father is incredibly powerful and surpasses all our enemies. His love for us knows no bounds. In times of hardship, it is essential to seek Him and place our trust in Him.

Although we may face challenges even as we pray and glorify God, we must never let it hinder our devotion to Him.

David teaches us valuable lessons on facing challenges by turning to God in gratitude, even in difficult times. When we keep our eyes on God, our problems seem smaller in comparison.

March 14

Isaiah 44:3

When we embrace Jesus as our Savior and have a deep longing for our Lord, we transform into a mighty wellspring of healing within our family, extending our influence to future generations. Our hearts are filled with the Holy Spirit, and we are blessed with divine power.

Love is the most precious gift we can offer to those in our lives. God, who is Love, has graciously given us this extraordinary blessing through our Lord Jesus Christ. Even if our loved ones or friends do not believe in Jesus, we can still demonstrate His presence within us and the miracles He can perform.

The key to satisfying our spiritual thirst lies in turning to Jesus, who offers us living water that will quench our thirst forever. By embracing Him, our souls will finally find the fulfillment they have been yearning for.

Sometimes the world may feel like a barren desert, with no hope in sight. However, it's necessary to remember that appearances can be deceiving. In such times, it's wise to look within and follow the guidance of the Holy Spirit, as it will always lead us to abundance and victory.

March 15

Luke 9:23

If we decide to follow Jesus, He instructs us to pick up our cross every day and walk in His footsteps. This means being mindful of our choices and putting in effort to live according to His teachings.

This passage illustrates that transformation is not an instant process, but rather a continual process. We need to make the conscious decision to prioritize our relationship with Him each morning and every moment of the day, putting aside our own selfish desires.

As we start to shift our focus from pursuing our own desires to seeking God's will first, we embark on a journey of constantly turning away from sin, crucifying our sinful selves, and embracing the ways of Jesus.

Going through this journey may be challenging, but the outcome is everlasting. We are fortunate to have the opportunity to be guided as cherished children of God and partake in His purity, which ultimately leads to a magnificent glory that surpasses any hardships we may face.

The invitation from Christ is always open, and it's our choice to answer. If your load becomes too heavy, just remember that your Savior is ready and willing to help. All you have to do is ask.

March 16

John 14:26

Before surrendering my life to Jesus, I can vividly recall a period when I was trapped in the clutches of addiction. Despite being surrounded by people, I experienced an overwhelming sense of loneliness and had no sense of direction in my life.

The day I made the decision to accept Jesus as my Savior is forever etched in my memory. The overwhelming sense of His presence brought tears to my eyes, and from that moment on, I knew I would never be alone again, and I could always seek His guidance.

It's been more than a decade now, and I've been running towards Him nonstop ever since. Despite facing numerous giants after surrendering to Jesus, I now confidently use the stones of God's word to defeat them and walk in victory like never before.

I may not carry my Bible everywhere, but I rely on the Holy Spirit to guide me in remembering who Jesus is and to bring God's word to mind throughout the day. The Holy Spirit speaks to my conscience, alerting me when something feels off.

It's crucial to pay attention to these nudges and to follow His guidance. Trust that God will always steer you in the right direction. When you feel lost and alone, look within yourself - you'll discover everything you ever need and more.

March 17

Romans 5:10

It’s easy to love someone when they are living in a way that seems pleasing to us. However, when they are living in a way that we don’t agree with, it becomes a bit more challenging. We may even decide to walk away altogether.

Praise God that He not only decided to shower us with His unwavering love even in our darkest moments, but also bestowed upon us His beloved son whom He cherishes deeply, as a sacrificial offering, to atone for our transgressions and pave the path towards reconciliation.

Before embracing Jesus as our Savior, we were all rebels, braving the wrath of God. But now, knowing that God has shown us mercy even in our sinfulness and granted us a new lease on life, we can only imagine the incredible things He will do for us now that we have reconciled with Him!

It's important to remember that by following God’s example, we should strive to show love to those who may be difficult to love and lead them towards Christ.

While it may be challenging, let's remember that even Jesus faced hardships on the cross, yet He still chose to love unconditionally.

Genesis 2:16-17

As caring parents, when we advise our children with statements such as, "Avoid playing in the street," or, "Stay away from drugs," we understand that we are providing this guidance for their well-being.

However, children being children may occasionally challenge our rules and regrettably learn through firsthand experience why these precautions are necessary.

Adam and Eve were lovingly warned by God in the garden, yet they decided not to trust His word, leading to the consequences that humanity has been facing ever since.

It's important to understand that we can have complete faith in every single word of the Bible, every loving promise from our Heavenly Father, and every warning mentioned in each chapter. Our role is not to doubt, but to wholeheartedly trust and follow.

Trusting in ourselves instead of placing our trust in God will result in a form of death every single time. God desires nothing but the best for us and wants us to experience a life filled with purpose and satisfaction, but ultimately, the decision lies in our hands.

March 19

Psalms 23:4

I can still recall the long ride to prison, bound in chains, gazing out the window, mentally preparing myself for the years I had to serve behind bars, so I prayed to God for protection and for the time ahead to bring healing.

As we arrived at the parking lot, the sight before me was exceedingly overwhelming. The towering razor wire encircled the buildings, while inmates and officers marched in an orderly line from one unit to another. Their curious gazes were fixed upon me, trying to see who the newcomer was.

As we stepped into the intake building, I sent up a final prayer to God and took a deep breath. I made a conscious effort to push aside my fears and surrender them completely to Him.

Throughout the seven years I spent behind bars, I faced numerous obstacles, yet not a single strand of hair on my head was ever touched. Amidst the constant chaos that surrounded me, I held onto a profound belief that God was watching over me. He had brought me this far for a reason, and I refused to give up now. With His guidance, I knew I had nothing to fear.

Keep walking in the light of His presence, and fear will have no place in your heart, no matter how deep the valley may seem.

Isaiah 29:15

If we believe that we can conceal our thoughts, intentions, or deeds from the Lord, we are merely deceiving ourselves. The Lord was aware of every aspect of our lives well before we even came into existence.

It's understandable if this fact seems a little invasive, but in the end, it serves as a compass for all our choices, helping to keep us on the narrow path.

When people decide to go their own way instead of following God's will, they are essentially conveying to God that they know better than He does. This rebellious and disobedient behavior can result in disastrous consequences.

This passage serves as a cautionary message, offering valuable guidance with the hope that we will opt to stay in the realm of truth rather than concealing our actions in the shadows. Eventually, everything will be revealed, and we will be held accountable for our choices.

Pray to the Lord for a heart overflowing with love and for growth through His grace. This way, we will lead lives that align with the state of our hearts.

March 21

Matthew 5:44

If you're breathing, chances are you've encountered a few individuals who aren't fond of you. Unfortunately, there will always be someone who harbors dislike towards us, regardless of their reasons. However, this doesn't release us from our duty to pray for them or to extend them grace.

God's grace is bestowed upon us even during our most challenging days. It is His desire for us to pass on the blessings we receive to those around us. As we strengthen our faith and become more courageous, we may encounter resistance and opposition from others, much like Jesus did.

Even in the midst of His suffering on the cross, Jesus offered a heartfelt prayer to our loving Father, asking Him to forgive those who were responsible for His crucifixion. His words, "forgive them for they know not what they do," (Luke 23:34) were a testament to His incredible compassion and forgiveness.

Jesus' prayer extended not only to those who crucified Him but to all sinners, demonstrating His boundless love even in the face of immense pain and suffering.

We can show love because God loved us first. Let's honor God by spreading His grace and love to those who may be difficult to love.

March 22

John 13:14-15

This passage beautifully portrays the qualities of an exemplary leader. Jesus, our Lord, King, Savior, and God Himself, humbly takes on the role of a servant by washing His disciples' soiled feet. It is a truly remarkable display of genuine love and compassion.

Jesus aimed to impart to His disciples the importance of those in positions of authority taking on the responsibility of humbly serving and caring for others. Furthermore, this act represented their role within the body of Christ.

Jesus not only spoke about His beliefs, but He also lived them out. His actions aligned perfectly with His words. It is a great example for all of us to strive towards. Our words and deeds should always mirror our faith in the Lord, just as Jesus' did in His unwavering faith in His Heavenly Father.

As we go about our daily lives, it is important for others to be drawn to the radiant light that emanates from within us. Our mere presence should have the power to dispel any darkness, as we allow Jesus to work through us and illuminate the world around us.

March 23

Acts 19:11

Paul's narrative is a blend of tragedy and an uplifting testament that reaffirms the belief that no individual is beyond redemption and can always find their way back to Jesus.

Initially, Paul embarked on a mission to suppress the dissemination of the gospel and relentlessly persecuted Jesus' disciples. His heart was calloused towards the teachings of Jesus, and his objective was to quash it entirely.

Paul, also known as Saul, had his initial personal encounter with God while traveling to Damascus. However, this encounter was far from comfortable. In fact, it was so powerful that it brought him to his knees and left him temporarily blinded. This life-altering experience completely transformed the trajectory of his life.

Paul started off as an adversary of God, but eventually became one of God's greatest supporters and demonstrations of His transformative power. A true testament to the fact that love can soften even the toughest of hearts.

God performed amazing miracles through Paul, so just think about what He can do through you! Let's keep praying for those who haven't met Jesus yet to have a life changing encounter with Him.

March 24

John 16:33

Life is full of challenges that are bound to come our way. Unfortunately, we don't possess a magical crystal ball that allows us to foresee the future and prepare ourselves accordingly or even avoid troubles altogether.

However, there is a glimmer of hope in the form of a Mighty Savior who has already paved the way for us, assuring us of victory through Him. When we choose to stay connected to Him, we find a sense of peace that transcends our circumstances.

Becoming like Christ doesn't guarantee a smooth journey. We will encounter challenges along the way, but how we choose to confront these obstacles determines the result. Will we rely on our own strength or place our faith in the Lord, even when we don't fully understand?

Satan has already faced defeat, yet he will attempt to deceive you and make you question God's word and promises. However, neither death nor Satan have the ultimate authority. God does. Remember, this life is temporary, and we are being prepared for eternal glory.

Although we may experience suffering now, it pales in comparison to what awaits us! It is crucial to remain rooted in God's word so that you can confidently stand against the lies of the devil.

March 25

Romans 12:18

After spending a few years in prison, I was assigned to share a room with a woman whom I didn't particularly like, and it was clear that the feeling was mutual.

We may not have seen things the same way most of the time, but we did share one common belief: we didn't want our situation to become any more difficult than it already was.

As I started to unpack my things, she mentioned, "I'm happy it's you who got moved into the room. You're quiet and you're clean, and you don't steal." I replied, "I know you're the same. Let's make the most of it. We've both been here a while, so we know it could be worse."

Because we shared a common belief in God and had both learned the importance of handling our issues maturely, we were able to set aside our differences and prioritize Jesus, making Him the center of our lives.

In life, there will inevitably be people who irritate us, but that doesn't give us an excuse to not act with kindness and strive for harmony. Revenge and anger are not our responsibilities; they belong to God Almighty. Our duty is to show love to others just as we have been loved by God.

March 26

Leviticus 20:26

Life consists of two main components: God's ultimate authority and our human influence. Through His grace, God sets us apart, sanctifies us, and molds us into His likeness.

By purifying ourselves and rejecting our selfish, sinful ways, we allow God to work through us, shining His light in the darkness of the world. This necessitates obedience, faith, and a great deal of diligence, and serves as a clear indication of spiritual growth.

We are fortunate to have the Holy Spirit guiding us like a compass on the right path. It's important for us to play our part in this journey. Although we may fall sometimes, holding onto Jesus' hand will help us rise again and bring glory to God.

It's incredibly amazing that the Almighty Creator has personally chosen you! He's extending an invitation for a close relationship with Him and a path to holiness.

Embracing His offer means a chance for a new beginning, and a life filled with endless possibilities. While challenges may arise, the blessings far outweigh them.

March 27

Psalms 16:5

At some point in our lives, we have all experienced a sense of lacking. We yearn for more money, a larger house, a promotion at work, a perfect marriage, or even recognition. It's common to feel that no matter how much effort we put in, we still fall short somehow.

The issue with this perspective lies in our point of view. If you adopt this mindset, your value is focused on earthly rewards rather than recognizing the abundant inheritance you have in Jesus Christ.

In the Bible, there are numerous accounts of individuals who patiently waited for years to witness the fulfillment of God's promises. Despite enduring various challenges and difficulties, they all shared a common understanding - that the Lord Himself was their ultimate source of fulfillment and blessings, regardless of their circumstances.

By shifting our perspective and acknowledging God as our ultimate source of fulfillment and provision, we find true contentment in knowing that He is everything we ever need.

Rather than constantly seeking more, take a moment today to appreciate the abundant blessings you have already received and express gratitude to God for all that He has bestowed upon you.

Matthew 7:7-8

The scripture emphasizes the importance of persistence. It demands a significant amount of energy, time, concentration, and unwavering determination. However, it is imperative that our endeavors are in accordance with God's word and His divine plan; otherwise, all our efforts will be in vain.

This passage serves as a gentle reminder that prayer serves as a direct line of communication between our hearts and the heart of God. It brings to light the fact that God truly cherishes those moments when we set aside some precious alone time with Him, shutting out the distractions of the world.

He is the one we should turn to first, sharing our needs and desires from the depths of our hearts. As we continue to mature in God's grace and understanding of His desires, it is vital that we constantly seek His presence.

The Lord has made a divine promise to grant us opportunities and blessings, but only if they align with His perfect will. Let us remain steadfast in our pursuit of Him, knowing that He will open doors of favor and abundance along our journey.

March 29

Malachi 3:17

God has a master plan in motion, a divine purpose for His beloved people. His ultimate goal is to guide those who once lived in defiance back to their true home with Him. We are His cherished treasures, held close to His heart.

Our compassionate Heavenly Father has been eagerly awaiting our return, showing immense patience and understanding, ensuring that no one is left behind and that everyone is given the chance to find their way back home.

There is a clear difference between those who dedicate themselves to God and those who do not. God is looking for people who live their lives in a unique way compared to the rest of the world. As children of God, it is our responsibility to live in a manner that is perceived by the world as different, vibrant, and filled with hope.

Even though our actions may appear insignificant in the grand scheme of things, God sees and values each one of them. Despite facing mockery from non-believers, God cherishes and acknowledges all our efforts done in His name, promising us a glorious and everlasting reward in the end.

March 30

Luke 10:19

This passage serves as a potent reminder that by choosing to carry our cross and walk in the footsteps of Jesus, we inevitably become formidable adversaries of the devil and his demonic followers. Their ultimate aim is not only to wreak havoc upon our lives, but also to condemn our souls to eternal damnation.

The effectiveness of a soldier hinges on the equipment they wield, the guidance of their leader, and their adherence to orders. A diligent soldier must always ready themselves for combat, therefore as Christian warriors, it is crucial to put on the full armor of God every morning in preparation for the daily struggles ahead.

In times of adversity and when faced with opposition, God reminds us that we have been equipped with the strength to emerge victorious in every struggle. It may seem overwhelming, but remember that the power within us is greater than any force in the world.

We should rely on the Lord's might, recognize our place in the body of Christ, and understand that the enemy has already been conquered. No challenge is insurmountable for us or for God. Stand firm in faith, unafraid, knowing that victory is already yours!

Romans 14:12

As adults, it is unrealistic to expect that young children possess the same knowledge as us. They have not yet acquired the life experience or education that we have, but nevertheless, we exhibit kindness, love, patience, and understanding towards them as they develop and learn.

As we continue to mature in our faith and understanding of the Lord, it's important to remember that we are all at different stages in our spiritual journey. Showing kindness, love, patience, and understanding towards one another is just as important as it is when dealing with a young child.

We are now all part of the same family, therefore those who have progressed further in their spiritual journey should take care of the newer members as if they were looking after a younger sibling. We must ensure that we do not lead anyone astray.

It's vital to remember our personal duty to honor our Father above everything else. We must be conscious of our actions and encourage others to do the same. Our job isn't to take on the role of our Father, but to support one another with love and grace, knowing that we will all answer to God in the end.

April

Ecclesiastes 4:9-12

Living a life tucked away in a corner is not what we were created for. We are designed for connection, companionship, and camaraderie. By surrounding ourselves with others, we can navigate challenges together and receive support when we need it.

We can find comfort in knowing that if we start to stray off path, there will be someone there to gently guide us back, as we all need a little help sometimes.

Sharing our experiences with others adds depth and richness to our lives. Giving blessings is just as fulfilling as receiving them. It's equally important to share our happiness as well as our struggles.

It's completely normal to crave solitude every now and then. Taking a moment to recharge and connect with God through prayer is essential for our well-being. Just like Jesus, finding time to be alone to pray can be truly refreshing.

If you have yet to discover your church community, I strongly urge you to prioritize finding one. Surrounding yourself with fellow believers who share your values is crucial. Remember, you are not meant to navigate through life alone; you are destined for so much more!

1 Corinthians 16:13

It may be hard to believe, but the challenges we face in life actually bring us blessings in the form of personal growth and resilience. By overcoming these trials with our faith, we gain valuable rewards that stay with us for a lifetime.

These trials act as a workout for our spiritual strength, increasing our faith and deepening our understanding of our Savior, ultimately preparing us for the next obstacle that comes our way.

Life's challenges may seem daunting, but we can navigate them by staying vigilant, holding onto our faith, and showing strength and courage. The Bible is full of stories where God's chosen people triumphed using these very strategies against all odds.

To maintain unwavering faith, we must stay firmly grounded in the rich soil of God's word. It is necessary to continuously renew our minds, allowing the sustenance of His word to strengthen our spirits and bolster our determination.

The strength mentioned here surpasses mere physical might; it pertains to fortifying our faith, as it will undoubtedly be tested. We must firmly anchor our faith and hope in Jesus, for life is far too short to live imprisoned within the walls of fear.

April 3

Proverbs 22:24-25

This passage is quite clear and direct. It cautions us about the dangers of associating with individuals who have a hot temper.

Not only do we put ourselves in harm's way by potentially becoming targets of their anger, but we also run the risk of adopting their volatile behavior.

As children of God, we shouldn't be running around angry all the time, creating chaos and unrest wherever we go. Being hot-tempered makes a person unpredictable.

Instead, we should strive to be predictable by showcasing qualities like peace, understanding, patience, and love in every situation we encounter. This can be quite challenging and requires a great deal of dedication to master.

If we refuse to embrace forgiveness and instead cling to anger, we create an opportunity for the devil to infiltrate our hearts and cause chaos not only in our own lives but also in the lives of those around us.

Choose wisely those who you allow to influence you. Surround yourself with those who motivate you to be more like Jesus. Through this, you will become a source of inspiration for others.

Isaiah 43:1

I'm not sure about you, but I've been called many names throughout my life. It seems like the world takes pleasure in trying to convince you to accept every negative label it throws your way. Its ultimate goal is to cloud your perception in an attempt to make you forget your true identity.

Our identity is not defined by our circumstances, or the hurtful words others may use against us. God has bestowed upon us an eternal name, a name that surpasses any name the world may try to label us with. It is important for us to rise above the falsehoods of the world and embrace the love of God, seeing ourselves as He sees us.

Satan's ultimate goal is to make us feel insignificant and abandoned. He will stop at nothing to make us believe that we are alone, unloved, and defeated. Through our struggles, he will try to deceive us into thinking that God has forsaken us.

Jesus endured immense suffering in anticipation of the joy that awaited Him. Likewise, we will face trials for the sake of the joy that lies ahead. The enemy's efforts to deceive us only highlight our significance. We are called by our God given name, and it is our choice to surrender to God, reject the devil, and embrace the forgiveness offered through Jesus' sacrifice.

April 5

Numbers 5:5-7

Our loving God is aware of our hidden sins, and we will ultimately be held accountable for them, whether it is in this life or the next. Whenever we engage in sinful acts, it signifies a lack of faithfulness and loyalty towards God.

When we make mistakes, the Lord wants us to take two important steps: admitting our faults and taking responsibility to rectify them. By openly confessing our wrongdoings to others and offering prayers for each other, we not only foster healing and restoration but also show reverence to God.

When I was young, I remember when a friend of my parents brought a paintball gun over. He handed it to me and said, "Go ahead, shoot the tree!" With my small and trembling hands, I pulled the trigger, but unfortunately, the paintball missed its target and splattered all over the freshly painted back door of our neighbors. I was absolutely terrified!

I had no choice but to gather my courage, walk to their house, and confess about the mess I had unintentionally created. Although they were not pleased, they were understanding and didn't treat me harshly. I understood the importance of taking responsibility for my actions, and I decided to do the right thing by using my allowance to cover the cost of new paint for their door.

April 6

Exodus 15:2

Countless times, people expressed their fears to me that I wouldn't make it out alive during my struggle with addiction. And honestly, I can't blame them for thinking that way.

Throughout my struggle with addiction, I found myself facing the terrifying reality of having guns pointed at me, associating with dangerous criminals, and subjecting my body to excessive amounts of drugs. It is nothing short of a miracle that I am alive today.

I realize that God was watching over me, even during my darkest moments. Despite facing challenges, I managed to overcome them all.

Since then, God has taken my darkness and used it to spread a message of light in the world around me, offering hope to those who are facing similar strugglcs as I did.

Despite my regrets over the decisions I've made, I am eternally thankful to the Lord for pulling me out of my despair and providing me with redemption. I will continuously share His love and compassion with anyone open to receiving it, giving Him thanks each day for being my rock, shield, rescuer, and my all in all.

The same God who delivered me is the same God who can deliver you. All you have to do is cry out.

April 7

Deuteronomy 8:10

It's human nature to become complacent in our daily routines when everything is going smoothly. We tend to turn to God only when we face hardships or tragedies that humble us. However, it's important to remember that God wants us to acknowledge Him even when we are content and grateful for the blessings we often overlook.

It's important to keep in mind that all the good things in our lives come from God. While we may be working hard and putting in long hours to earn a good salary, it is God who has bestowed upon us good health and blessings, allowing us to have our jobs and provide for ourselves and our loved ones.

All the money we possess, all the food stocked in our pantry, every trip we go on, each functioning appliance in our home, every positive connection we have, our homes, vehicles, clothes - they are all valuable blessings from our gracious God. The only thing He desires in return is a little gratitude and recognition.

Let's remember to appreciate the wonderful blessings we have in our lives every day. They serve as a lovely reminder of the care and attention to detail that our Lord gives us. Our freedom to worship and connect with God is a beautiful gift. It's important to acknowledge that everything we have is because of Him!

April 8

Job 1:8

If you were to lose everyone and everything you hold dear today, would you still choose to honor, love, and stay faithful to God? Even after dedicating your whole life to being a humble and faithful servant?

Satan approached God, and God acknowledged that there was no servant as faithful as Job. Job was a righteous and honorable man, who despised evil and held a deep reverence for God.

However, Satan challenged Job's devotion, suggesting that it was solely based on the blessings he received from God. In response, God permitted Satan to strip away all of Job's possessions, but He forbade Satan from taking Job's life.

Job's unwavering faith and devotion to the Lord remained unshaken despite the heart-wrenching ordeal of losing his children, home, servants, and livestock, and enduring physical afflictions.

Job was blessed by God with even greater abundance in his later years than before. Although it can't replace what he had lost, God provided him with a new beginning after enduring immense hardship. It is crucial to praise God during every storm, having faith that this difficult time will eventually come to an end.

April 9

Ezekiel 18:31-32

God has blessed us with a guiding compass through His word, yet He has also granted us the freedom to choose our own path. It's our decision whether to heed His guidance or venture down our own path.

Our caring Father desires the best for us, hoping that we will abandon our self-centered, sinful behaviors and seek forgiveness. He understands that if we persist on our current course, we will inevitably encounter ruin and death. His wish is for us to embrace a renewed life through the grace provided by Jesus Christ.

God is the ultimate judge, yet it is our decisions that ultimately bring about judgement. He is loving, merciful, and empathetic, ready to offer grace to those who seek it by turning to Him and abandoning their sinful ways.

If you haven't placed your complete trust in Jesus for the forgiveness of your sins, why not do it today? He has the power to save you. Jesus has triumphed over sin and death, defeating the grave, and He extends this victory to you through His blood. Ask the Lord to help guide you away from temptation, enabling you to experience life to the fullest.

April 10

Daniel 4:2

Brace yourself for the incredible impact that God's presence can have on your life. This verse beautifully illustrates the life-altering power that comes with His arrival. When God makes His grand entrance, prepare to be amazed because everything changes in the most extraordinary way!

It never fails to amaze me how people react when they meet me now, especially after they've heard about my past. Without fail, they all say, "I can't believe that was you!" Even those who used to know me say the exact same thing. And every time, I respond with a simple truth, "It was God who transformed me."

Having experienced the life-altering power of my incredible God, my sole desire became to spread awareness of what He is capable of, so that everyone could have their own profound encounter with Him. When you encounter such boundless love and mercy, it's impossible not to want to share it with others.

Every day, I take a moment to reflect on my life and I am truly amazed at how much I have achieved with the help of the Lord. Your story about God is a beacon of hope for others to find their way to our Heavenly Father.

April 11

Hosea 6:6

God wants more from us than just going through the motions of religious duty. He wants us to offer our hearts and show genuine love and devotion to Him. He desires a deep connection with us, not just superficial actions like attending church occasionally, reciting empty prayers, and giving a small donation here and there.

Everyone yearns for a love that is genuine, authentic, and unwavering. The same goes for God, who also longs for such profound connections.

None of us desire to be in a relationship that lacks passion and commitment, where both parties only make the bare minimum effort to stay connected. Such relationships are not only a waste of time and energy but also inflict immense pain.

God gazes upon us with eyes full of hope, seeing beyond our flaws to the potential we hold through the selfless act of Jesus Christ. His love for us knows no bounds, as He spares no effort in guiding us back to where we truly belong - in His loving embrace.

Make it a daily practice to deepen your connection with Him by delving into His teachings and demonstrating your unwavering devotion.

April 12

Jeremiah 10:23-24

It can be quite discouraging to look around us and see people choosing to live in chaos, civil unrest, and division, making choices that do not align with the teachings of God. Despite our best efforts, there will always be those who refuse to listen and choose their own path instead.

In times like these, our best course of action is to humbly seek God's guidance, trusting Him to steer us on the right path. While we can only control ourselves, it's important to acknowledge our dependence on God and His wisdom. Let us remain steadfast and open to His correction, for He alone can keep us on the narrow path He has chosen for us.

Fortunately, we are blessed with a caring Father who is lovingly attentive and willing to help. He is always there for us, ready to listen, understand, and take action. We are privileged to have direct access to Him, allowing us to approach Him with humility and request His guidance in examining our hearts and purifying us from our wicked ways.

Let us surrender everything to the Lord and rely on Him to carry the weight of our past, present, and future. Instead of trying to navigate life on our own, let's stay focused on Him and persevere with unwavering faith.

April 13

Psalms 6:6

Depression is a tangible experience. It can completely engulf us, making us believe that we are being punished by God or abandoned by Him. A sense of hopelessness can take hold, and negative thoughts can constantly swirl in our minds, even disrupting our sleep and worsening our exhaustion and depression.

During these times, it's crucial for us to dive into God's word and hold on tightly to His promises. He assures us that He will always be with us, no matter what, and even though we may face challenges, we can find peace knowing that He has already conquered them, and this difficult time will eventually pass.

We are never alone, unloved, unwanted, or worthless. The devil constantly tries to deceive us with lies, hoping to trap us in the grip of depression and lead us towards thoughts of suicide. However, our Father has blessed us with life so that we may experience it abundantly.

When the dark cloud of depression looms over us, we can find solace and strength in Him above all else. By holding onto the truth of God's word, we can banish the evil spirit of depression from our lives. So, let us continue to cry out to the Lord, knowing that He will answer us in His perfect timing.

April 14

1 Chronicles 16:12

Yesterday, we delved into the topic of depression, and today's verse perfectly complements it. Picture this: the men in the boat, facing a ferocious storm that seemed ready to engulf them. Amidst the chaos, there was Jesus, peacefully asleep.

The men were driven to awaken Jesus, as if He had no knowledge of the raging storm. However, the reality was that He remained undisturbed, for He had complete faith that despite the severity of the storm, they would reach the other side unharmed. It seemed they had overlooked the fact that the Almighty was right there with them in the boat.

They had come a long way with God by their side, and He wasn't going to abandon them now. Despite overcoming many challenges in life, they almost gave up when faced with this particular obstacle, relying on what they could see rather than the undeniable truth before them.

There isn't a single storm in your life that God isn't capable of handling. He promises to stand by your side through every trial. No fear, depression, or hopelessness can alter this truth. It's important to stop trusting everything you see and instead, focus on who God is in your life. He has guided you this far, and He will continue to lead you into eternity.

April 15

Exodus 14:14

This particular scripture holds a special place in my heart, as it serves as a constant reminder for me. It emphasizes the significance of finding stillness and allowing God to take charge, rather than interfering and attempting to control every situation.

It teaches me that not everything is within my realm of responsibility. I must admit, I am someone who thrives on action and productivity. Sitting idly and waiting for things to unfold is not my strong suit. I prefer to swiftly tackle my to-do list, ensuring that I can move on to the next task before it becomes overwhelming.

Every day, I make a conscious effort to remember that God has already paved the path for me. All I have to do is have faith in His divine plan, fulfill my responsibilities, and give Him the praise He deserves.

Remaining still does not necessarily imply being idle; rather, it entails recognizing what is within your control and what is in the hands of God. It requires a brave display of faith, where you grasp His hand and confidently declare, "We can handle this!" Regardless of the challenges you encounter, remember that God is your ultimate champion.

April 16

John 20:21

Even though Jesus has departed from this world physically, He has not abandoned us or left us without guidance. We are fortunate to have the Holy Spirit as our constant companion, providing us with guidance, comfort, and conviction.

Additionally, we have been bestowed with the precious gift of the Bible, which allows us to renew our hearts and minds each day, immersing ourselves in its profound truth.

We have been bestowed with a divine blessing and entrusted with a divine mission. The good news has reached our ears, and it is now our duty to spread it far and wide.

Your individuality makes you the ideal vessel through which God can touch someone's life and lead them towards salvation. Embrace your uniqueness and be the instrument of divine grace.

Jesus frequently withdrew to a quiet place to connect with God and experience peace and renewal. We can also discover these blessings by spending time alone with Him, but we are not meant to isolate ourselves from the world or avoid others. Instead, let this peace inspire us to serve the Lord and lead others to salvation.

April 17

1 John 4:18

Upon accepting Jesus Christ as our Savior, we are saved, and His blood covers all our sins - past, present, and future. We are made whole and perfect through God, not due to our own perfection, but because of His. God, who is Love, resides within us, and we in Him, and Love never fails.

We have all experienced moments of fear, however, the main objective of fear is to hinder your progress. Its aim is to prevent you from achieving the purpose that God has bestowed upon you. Fear is a deceitful force that seeks to undermine you by exploiting your insecurities.

To overcome fear, one must confront it head-on and act despite of fear. If you believe that you have been called to act, or if you sense the prompting of the Holy Spirit, rest assured that God will lead you to victory over any challenges that you face.

No matter what challenges you face, remember that the Lord is by your side, loving you with an invincible love. This knowledge brings the reassurance that the same unstoppable power resides within you, and no fear can stand against it.

April 18

Romans 12:10

There's a kind lady in my church who dedicates her time in the kitchen cooking and baking. After preparing her delicious treats, she goes around town delivering them to those who are in need of a meal - whether they are unwell, unable to cook for themselves, or facing financial difficulties.

Apart from baking for charitable causes, she also finds ways to support her community. She covers all the costs herself, but what really drives her is her love for serving the Lord. It's not out of duty, but out of a genuine heart filled with God's love.

Witnessing her unwavering devotion to the Lord and her selfless acts of honoring others has been a beautiful and inspiring experience for me. It motivates me to serve God by wholeheartedly serving others with passion and dedication.

You never know the impact you may have on others or the inspiration you may provide simply by being yourself and using your God given talents to make the world a better place, all while honoring God.

Your obedience has a ripple effect, spreading healing waves that touch the lives of those around you.

Luke 3:11

Sharing is not a new concept, and it's not always the most welcomed thing to do either. However, taking care of others' needs is a fundamental principle of following Jesus.

The message provided in this passage is straightforward. If you have more than enough, extend a helping hand to those who are lacking. Genuine faith goes beyond mere words; it is exemplified through our actions and obedience.

When I lived in New Orleans briefly, I ventured downtown to seek assistance. As I entered the building, the sight of the homeless with their tattered clothing caught in the fence holes greeted me. The line at the food kitchen stretched as far as the eye could see, filled with people patiently waiting for what might be their only meal of the day.

In that moment, I offered a heartfelt prayer for them, expressing gratitude to God for those generous souls who donated their time and money to support the less fortunate. It also made me appreciate the little we had at that time, instilling in me a profound gratitude for the blessings in my own life.

The blessings of God don’t end with you, it’s where they begin.

April 20

Ephesians 1:7

It is solely by the shed blood of Jesus that we are granted access to Heaven. It deeply saddens me whenever I reflect on the immense suffering He endured for our sake. Our redemption was His utmost devotion. His love for His loved ones meant more to Him than His own life.

When Jesus covered our debt, it went beyond what we typically think of as debt. Unlike buying a house or a car, where we eventually have the chance to pay it off, the debt Jesus paid was one we could never fully repay. It was a debt that would always remain unpaid.

Without the blood of Jesus, our connection with God would be eternally severed. Love is the essence of God, and without it, our lives would be empty. Just think about a world devoid of love! Since God is holy, it is essential for us to strive for holiness as well.

The good news is that we are loved beyond measure, and all our sins from the past, present, and future have been completely forgiven! God, in His abundant grace, has made certain that we are completely covered. This incredible gift is freely given by our caring Father, and all we have to do is accept it.

April 21

Philippians 2:14-16

The scripture teaches us that to become blameless and pure, we should avoid complaining or arguing while doing things. This means refraining from voicing our complaints and also keeping a positive attitude in our hearts towards God.

Doing the dishes has never been my cup of tea. Whether it was during my childhood or as an adult, I always despised this chore. Back in the day, I would attempt to pass the responsibility onto my younger brother, and as I grew older, I would often try to convince my spouse to take over this dreaded task. However, my perspective changed when I found Jesus.

When God revealed to me the many blessings He had given, I found myself filled with gratitude while washing the dishes. I expressed thanks for the meals we prepared and enjoyed, for the loved ones gathered around the table, for my health and ability to clean, for the water that washed the dishes, for the roof over our heads that stored them, and most importantly, for a loving God who granted me this moment to appreciate even the dirty dishes.

There are countless reasons to be grateful, and when we fully acknowledge all the blessings God has bestowed upon us, there is no room left for anything other than thankfulness and praise.

April 22

Exodus 20:4-6

God understands that we will face temptations and be lured towards sinful desires, but He instructs us to prioritize Him above everything else and worship Him alone. He views idolatry as a serious offense because it diminishes His glory. All the blessings we receive are gifts from Him and Him alone.

Anything can become a false God if we prioritize it over our one true God. Whether it's money, drugs, sex, gambling, food, a person, video games, or anything else, it's important to reflect on whether we would sin to hold onto it and if we are dedicating more time and energy to it than to God Himself.

God is jealous for us, but His jealousy is not like human jealousy. It is His desire to protect what rightfully belongs to Him and to ensure our well-being. He knows that if we choose to go astray, it will only lead to negative consequences and even death.

God has shown His love and commitment to you through Christ, hoping that you will value the bond between you two and never allow anything to disrupt it. Jesus is the assurance that you will be reunited with your true love in Heaven after this life ends.

April 23

Ezra 9:13

I recall a particular evening when my eldest son, who was a teenager at the time, asked to spend the night at his friend's house. They had been buddies for quite a while, and it was a common practice for them to take turns sleeping over at each other's homes. Naturally, I agreed and went on with the rest of my evening.

After a few hours, there was a knock on the door, so I went to see who it was. To my surprise, it was my son's friend looking for him. It dawned on me that I had been tricked. I had his friend call him to figure out his whereabouts, all while secretly listening in.

Upon discovering that he was attending an overnight party, his friend got in my car, and we proceeded to the party venue. As soon as my son realized that he had been caught, he made no attempt to argue. He simply got in the car, admitted his deception, and we drove back home.

Despite my initial anger and disappointment, I found solace in the fact that he was unharmed. Instead of losing my temper, we had a heartfelt discussion, and I imposed a short grounding. This situation reminded me of our relationship with God when we admit our wrongdoings and seek forgiveness. He readily forgives us and guides us on the way everlasting.

April 24

Psalms 37:4

God's promise in this scripture is truly amazing. He understands our deepest desires and longs for us to experience a life overflowing with blessings through His grace. The key thing to remember is that we must find joy in Him above all else.

Spending time with God transforms us from the inside out. As we grow in our love and knowledge of Him, our hearts, minds, and lives are renewed. Our desires start to align more closely with His will, and we can trust that He will grant our requests that are in line with His perfect plan.

Throughout the seven years I spent in prison, an incredible transformation took place within me, thanks to the divine intervention of God. His work in my life surpassed all expectations, molding me into a completely different person.

I began to pray, seeking a godly husband, and soon realized that God had a plan in mind. Before granting my request, He wanted to ensure that I was ready to embrace the role of a godly wife.

It was truly amazing how God answered my prayer and brought him into my life at just the right moment, in a way that completely surprised me. But it wasn't until I found joy in the Lord and let Him work in my life that I understood the value of my answered prayer.

April 25

Hosea 14:9

Sin is a grave matter that should not be taken lightly. It is akin to betraying our divine spouse, God. It presents us with a pivotal decision - whether to remain faithful to our beloved or to stray away.

Despite our transgressions, God's love for us, His cherished bride, knows no bounds. He was even willing to make the ultimate sacrifice to redeem and protect us.

In this passage, two paths are outlined: the path of the righteous and the path of the rebellious. You are faced with a decision, a fork in the road where you must either turn left or turn right. There is no alternative route, and you must make a choice. This decision is inescapable, for it shapes the course of your journey.

To stay in sync with God, it is vital to consistently refresh your mind with His word and pay attention to the gentle nudges of the Holy Spirit.

What you do or don’t do today, will not change what you did or didn’t do yesterday, but it will determine what you can or can’t do tomorrow.

April 26

Jonah 3:8

When we come to the realization that we need to repent and make a change in our lives, it has a profound impact on those around us. Our transformation serves as a powerful example, inspiring others to recognize their own need for repentance and to embark on their own journey of change.

By openly sharing the incredible things that God has done in our lives, we are not only recounting our personal experiences, but also extending a beacon of hope to those who are desperately seeking it.

Genuine repentance begins with listening to the teachings of God, acknowledging our faults, and leads to forsaking our old ways. Avoiding our mistakes is not a solution. Confronting them directly is the only way to move forward. If we evade the path that God has laid out for us, our lives will forever be plagued by turmoil.

When the Holy Spirit reveals our sins through Jesus Christ, the most appropriate reaction is to humbly confess to God, acknowledging our mistakes, and accept the forgiveness and blessings from our merciful Savior.

April 27

Habakkuk 2:14

We all find ourselves pondering over questions for God. It's natural to observe the world around us and feel a mix of emotions - overwhelmed, confused, and even frustrated - when we try to comprehend why certain things are allowed to persist. Life, at times, can be quite perplexing.

As our faith matures, we rely less on our own abilities and understanding, and instead, we place our trust in God and anchor our hope in Him. Believing in God's divine plan is the key to navigating through the challenges of a broken world.

There is always hope. Although challenges may arise before things improve, God has assured us that His glory will fill the entire Earth, not just a portion of it. His glory is powerful and will touch the lives of everyone. His light will shine through every darkness, eradicating it completely. Rest assured; God always keeps His promises.

In the future, Jesus will lovingly wipe away every tear from our eyes, and we will all come together, hand in hand, celebrating Him as a united and faithful bride. Until that day arrives, let us persistently pray for others and the state of this broken world. Let us remain steadfast in our faith, regardless of what our eyes may witness.

April 28

Haggai 1:13

You are a sacred temple, a dwelling place for the Almighty God Himself. His divine presence is forever intertwined with your being.

You are a sacred sanctuary that He is diligently restoring, as He tirelessly works within you to mend the wounds caused by sin and replace them with His miraculous restoration. He is the ultimate architect, crafting a masterpiece within you.

Have you ever stopped to ponder if we are genuinely making God our top priority, just as He has made us His? It's a thought-provoking question that can be answered by examining the evidence of our lives.

Take a moment to reflect on where and how you invest your time, money, and energy. Are your choices aligned with a life that revolves around God and His teachings?

We should shift our focus from questioning if God is with us to questioning if we are sincerely with God. It is important to take a moment today to reflect on our priorities and allow the Master Builder to continue to do His work in and through us.

May our lives serve as a clear reflection of God's presence at the core of our being.

April 29

Matthew 18:21-22

When we hold onto any feelings of unforgiveness in our hearts and minds, it ultimately only harms ourselves. It gradually eats away at our well-being until it completely consumes us. Unless we learn to master it, it will master us.

Forgiveness can be an incredibly challenging and humbling act, but according to this scripture, Jesus emphasizes the importance of extending forgiveness.

Just as the Lord has forgiven us, we are called to forgive others. By offering forgiveness, we free ourselves from the heavy burden it carries.

Jesus expressed immense love and compassion when, in His final moments on the cross, He asked God to forgive those responsible for His crucifixion.

It is truly remarkable to consider the depth of His love, as He endured unimaginable suffering and imminent death at the hands of those who betrayed Him, and still He chose to forgive.

God has given us the precious gift of love, which resides within our hearts. It is up to us to make the conscious decision to let it flow freely and drive out the darkness in this world.

Psalms 27:1

Trusting in the Lord can be challenging at times. It requires unwavering faith, perseverance, and resilience. During these moments, doubt may creep in, tempting you to think that God has abandoned you. However, rest assured that this couldn't be further from the truth.

God's love is an unbreakable bond that connects us to Him in all circumstances. Within us, His Holy Spirit provides peace and guidance, illuminating our path even in the darkest of times. Hope, salvation, and glory are found in Him alone.

Sometimes we may feel like we're at our breaking point, facing insurmountable challenges, but remember that God will provide us with the strength to persevere if we seek Him first. It's important not to rely solely on our own abilities.

We are continuously being refined and should be ready to surrender our all to the Lord, or else we will face significant suffering.

Trust in God's perfect timing, whether in moments of joy or pain. He has been your guiding light and will continue to support you. Remember, He has always been there to carry you through your struggles. There is no need to be afraid.

May

May 1

Proverbs 3:7

Prior to making any major decisions, I make sure to seek guidance from God through prayer. I trust that He has a better perspective on things and can provide me with the right path to follow, preventing me from making mistakes or losing my way.

It's always best to seek God's guidance when making decisions. What appears to be a great choice now could lead to trouble later on, while something that seems risky might actually turn out to be a blessing in disguise.

When we have reverence for God, everything else starts to align. We acknowledge that He is the ultimate giver and taker. Through His grace, we discover beauty and are spiritually nourished by His presence. We refrain from pursuing things that we know are not meant for us, and instead, we lead lives that bring glory to God.

The world and the devil may promote independence, but we can see from Adam and Eve’s story where that led. As human beings, we were designed for connection and reliance on our Heavenly Father.

Our need for Him will forever remain. Embracing a reverential fear of God forms the solid groundwork upon which true success is built.

Job 9:12

In this passage, Job eloquently portrays the magnificent authority of God. It is beyond human comprehension to challenge God's judgments or question His righteousness. The Almighty bestows blessings upon us and, if He so chooses, may also withdraw them.

Life is fleeting, filled with both blessings and heartaches that come and go in the blink of an eye. That's why it's important to embrace the present, appreciate the joys that God has bestowed upon us, and surrender any burdens to Him, knowing that through our struggles, we will find growth and strength.

It's completely normal to have moments in life where we wonder why things are happening the way they are. Remember to trust in God's plan instead of relying solely on our own understanding. Rest assured that He will work everything out for the best in the end.

When the weight of today's challenges becomes overwhelming, just remember to lift your gaze and find peace in the knowledge that the splendor of Heaven awaits you, embraced by the loving arms of our Heavenly Father.

May 3

Isaiah 35:8

We have been invited on a journey along the Heavenly Highway, a sacred route exclusively reserved for the redeemed, the ransomed of the Lord, and even the wandering souls seeking solace.

This extraordinary path leads to a privileged destination, where those who tread upon it shall witness the brilliance of God's glory and bask in the divine embrace of His presence.

Jesus will undoubtedly come back to gather what rightfully belongs to Him. The Holy Spirit will serve as a reliable and trustworthy guide until the moment of His return.

This remarkable journey begins on the day you wholeheartedly embrace Jesus Christ as your personal Savior, and it ends when you gracefully enter the gates of Heaven, reaching your eternal destination.

It is important to show patience and kindness towards yourself as you journey along this path. There will be numerous opportunities for personal growth as you continue moving forward, and the rewards will be priceless in the long run.

Luke 11:28

Jesus is very clear in His words. He mentions that those who listen and follow His teachings will be blessed. Those who hear the message of salvation and accept it with faith will receive a new life filled with grace from Jesus Christ.

As we demonstrate our trust and love for the Lord, obedience becomes a testament to our devotion. It requires us to prioritize our beloved above everything else, even our own fears and desires. Just like Jesus, who exemplified obedience until His crucifixion, we are called to fully surrender ourselves to God.

Growing in our relationship with the Lord allows us to be a beacon of hope for others as we share the message of forgiveness and salvation. Jesus is our hope and guide through all obstacles we face.

While life may not be without challenges, we can overcome them by placing our trust in God. By doing so, we not only shine with His light but also inspire others to seek that same light within themselves.

The word of God brings peace, and following it brings blessings. It is a source of love that emanates from its pages, guiding you towards a fulfilling life.

Romans 8:15

It is amazing how Love Himself has tirelessly pursued us. Take a moment to contemplate the extraordinary measures God has taken to reach out to you, and you will undoubtedly be filled with an immense and profound sense of awe.

We have been blessed with God's eternal Spirit, residing within us to provide strength and bring about a transformative impact on our lives. As we make our way back to Him, we are akin to wayward children, crossing the bridge of grace to find our way home.

The gift of His Spirit serves as a guarantee of our eternal home in Heaven. Just like Jesus encountered challenges, we too will face difficulties, but we can take comfort in knowing that just as Jesus triumphed, we will also prevail.

There is no need for fear on this journey of life. We are just travelers passing through. Life is the nurturing soil where we are planted to flourish, showered with blessings from our caring Lord in the form of sunshine and rain, providing us with all that we require.

May 6

Exodus 20:14

It is our duty to honor our bodies as sacred temples and ensure they are well taken care of, embodying the presence of God. The act of physical intimacy should be a manifestation of our devotion to God and should be reserved for the sanctity of marriage.

Marriage is a sacred bond with God, where two individuals become one. It is important to take this commandment seriously as it holds great significance not only in your physical marriage, but also a reflection of your union with the Lord.

Adultery not only breaks this covenant physically but also extends to the thoughts and desires we entertain. We must be vigilant in guarding ourselves against any form of adultery.

Indulging in sinful desires or thoughts is equivalent to committing adultery. This encompasses watching pornography, engaging in flirtatious behavior, and any suggestive behaviors. Always treat your partner the way you would want to be treated in return.

In the New Testament, Jesus reaffirms this belief in Matthew 5:27-29. To stay true to your faith, it is essential to anchor your life in the fertile ground of God's boundless love.

Joshua 1:8

Meditating on the teachings of God throughout the day and night is the pathway to receiving abundant blessings and provisions from Heaven.

By immersing oneself completely in the word of God, it permeates every facet of life. Rest assured, God has promised us that our faithfulness will be duly acknowledged and rewarded.

It's important to remember that following any path other than the one the Lord has planned for us will only bring devastation. Any achievements we may have outside of His will won't last long.

To truly succeed and prosper, we need to look to the word of God, read it, believe it, meditate on it, and follow it obediently.

The power of God's word is alive and constantly at work within us through the Holy Spirit. True success lies in discovering God's purpose for our lives and living in the abundance thereof.

If you haven't done so already, try to find a way to include reading your Bible in your daily morning and evening routine. You can keep a Bible by your bedside or utilize a Bible app on your phone. Allow God to bring you peace in the morning and be your source of peace at night.

Romans 15:7

I will always hold a special place in my heart for the church ladies who selflessly visited us inmates in the county jail. Despite knowing that they were entering a room filled with women from different backgrounds and with various criminal histories, their kindness and love never wavered. Their presence deeply impacted our lives, and for women such as me, led us to find redemption.

I witnessed the genuine heart of Jesus within those women. That's exactly how love should look. They helped me in recognizing my sin, seeking forgiveness, and leading me towards the path of redemption. After I found salvation, we became sisters in Christ and to this very moment, we continue to have heartfelt conversations over coffee.

I was warmly embraced by them and never felt like an outsider. Their acceptance taught me valuable lessons, which I now pass on to others, hoping to guide them towards finding solace in their faith. The love and grace I received from them enables me to love and extend grace to others in return.

When we love as Jesus loves, we destroy the barriers that divide us, and bring glory to God.

May 9

Luke 12:25

It's true that worry can take a heavy toll on us. It can drain our energy and leave us feeling exhausted in every way possible. Not only that, but it can also steal precious moments that could be spent enjoying life with those we care about. Worry has a way of clouding our minds and making us feel more sensitive and emotional than usual.

Spending so much time and effort worrying never actually alters the outcome in our favor or enhances our lives in any way. It's utterly pointless.

To conquer worry, the key lies in adopting a handful of effective strategies and consistently applying them until they become second nature.

We have the ability to do various things such as: Recalling the times when God has come through for you in the past, understanding that if something is meant for you, it will eventually be yours, having faith in God's plan, finding rest in His peace, and expressing gratitude to God while waiting.

Remember, you alone hold the power to prevent the devil from robbing you of your joy and peace.

May 10

Nahum 1:13

This passage reveals the incredible power and mercy of our Lord. He has the ability to shatter the chains that have held us captive in sin. Jesus was sent to us for this very purpose - to break the chains, open the door to freedom, and lead us back to our Heavenly Father.

It's important to remember that God desires for us to experience the blessings He has for us. He eagerly awaits to hear from us each day, hoping that we also seek to hear from Him. His love for us is beyond measure.

We should seek God's intervention and actively fulfill our responsibilities. He is always ready to confront the challenges that surround us, but it is our decision to remain in His light and not go back to the darkness that once held us captive.

Each challenge we encounter prepares us with the resilience and wisdom needed to overcome the next obstacle.

Trust that God is there to support you in facing the demons that come your way. He not only empowers you to fight back, but He will also ensure your victory and elevate you in His Kingdom!

May 11

Isaiah 1:18

Have you ever stepped outside on a crisp, sunny morning after a snowfall and been blinded by the brilliant glow of the sun bouncing off the pure white snow? This is how our sins will appear according to this scripture.

Once we embrace Jesus Christ as our Savior, His blood purifies every aspect of our being, both seen and unseen. God's actions are never half-hearted. He purifies us in a way that brings about a complete and remarkable transformation.

It's crucial to regularly assess our lives and relationships. Have you been feeling guilty about anything recently? Is there something you need to ask for forgiveness for? Remember, God is always there to listen, and if you confess your sins and turn away from them, He will cleanse you completely.

We all make mistakes, so if you feel like you've fallen countless times, don't forget that God still believes in you. While you're on your knees, say a prayer and reach out to the Lord's hand that is always extended to you with love, grace, and mercy.

Psalms 7:15

This passage is incredibly straightforward. Those who actively look for ways to harm others will ultimately only harm themselves. This is why it is essential to entrust vengeance to God.

Nothing occurs without the Lord's knowledge. No wrongdoing can be concealed or kept secret from Him. He observes every intention, understands every thought, and witnesses every action we take.

Rest assured, justice may not always arrive as swiftly as we desire in certain situations. However, we must remember that it will eventually prevail.

As children of the Most High God, it is our responsibility to control our anger, carefully consider our actions, and seek guidance from Him.

Our path should be one of righteousness, avoiding the detours of selfish desires and seeking revenge. These actions do not align with God's glory and only result in our own downfall.

Please remember to pray for discernment regarding the deceitful plans of the wicked. Ask the Lord to lead you safely away from them and seek His guidance on the lessons you are meant to learn from these experiences.

May 13

Joshua 1:9

Isn't it amazing how reassuring this command and promise is? We are encouraged to be courageous knowing that God is by our side every step of the way. Even though we may not have all the answers or know what the future holds, we can be confident in one thing: the Almighty is with us and for us!

It's important to remember that being strong and courageous doesn't always require a big show in front of others. Sometimes, it's about the small choices we make every day, demonstrating our trust in the Lord and following His example with unwavering faith.

When we find ourselves in a deep, dark valley, it may seem like we are all alone, but that couldn't be further from the truth. God is constantly by our side, guiding us through the challenges that lie ahead. All we need to do is have faith that He will lead us to the other side.

We must not succumb to fear! Fear only brings about a chain of regrets and unhappiness. Having courage and faith will always bring blessings and personal growth.

May 14

1 Corinthians 1:27-29

When I first heard the call to serve the Lord, I questioned why anyone would listen to me. But then, the Holy Spirit gently reassured me, saying, "Just follow my lead and I will handle the rest. You may encounter challenges, just like Jesus did, but your message and bravery will reach those who need it to expand my Kingdom."

Despite doubts and fears, I have willingly placed myself in vulnerable positions, sharing my voice and past experiences to bring hope to those in need.

It's absolutely awe-inspiring how God chooses ordinary individuals like myself, who have faced challenging pasts, to showcase the incredible strength of His light. This serves as a powerful reminder that no matter how dark our history may be, His light will always prevail.

It's a testament to the remarkable resilience of humanity, which is made possible by the grace of our Almighty Father. It's not about what we have done, but rather the immense power of His presence in our lives.

It's never really about us - it's always about God. He has chosen us to be vessels for tearing down strongholds. Never underestimate the incredible power that works within you.

May 15

Galatians 6:4

The ultimate standard by which we should judge ourselves is the word of God. It's important not to fall into the trap of comparing ourselves to others. Instead, we should constantly evaluate whether our words, actions, thoughts, and decisions align with what would please the Lord, as if He were right beside us at all times - because He is.

Comparing ourselves to others can lead to two outcomes: either we try to justify our actions by saying, "I'm not as bad as that person," or we feel jealous and envious, which can ultimately lead to bitterness and depression. Unfortunately, neither of these responses is beneficial or pleasing to God.

In this scripture, the spotlight is on the significance of owning up to our actions and concentrating on our relationship with the Lord, rather than seeking validation from others. It highlights the idea of living in a manner that reflects our faith and values, allowing our actions to speak louder than words.

By aligning ourselves with God's will and finding contentment in His approval alone, we can discover true joy and fulfillment. This scripture serves as a source of encouragement, empowering us to strengthen our faith journey.

May 16

Hebrews 12:7

The term discipline doesn't exactly evoke warm and fuzzy feelings within me. It's like my brain automatically links it to suffering, and I'm all about avoiding anything that causes me pain.

However, God has a different perspective on discipline than my automatic assumptions. His correction isn't about wrath or punishment. When He sees that we need to learn and grow from the sins we're entangled in, He guides us through a process that can be quite uncomfortable.

But it's important to remember that this process is always rooted in love, because God is our compassionate Father who desires what's truly best for us.

We can embrace discipline as proof that we are part of God's loving family. He treats us as His beloved children, guiding us with care and affection. Without His correction, we would be lost in a chaotic world.

Thankfully, we have the assurance that our Heavenly Father is constant and unwavering, always shaping us to reflect the image of Jesus more and more each day.

May 17

Psalms 18:46

Every morning, we should wake up and give thanks to the Lord, just like David did, for the victories God has brought into our lives and the assurance we have in Him for the future.

We can express our gratitude for God's unwavering strength and constant presence, which empowers us as we continue to deepen our understanding of Him.

The Lord is our immovable rock, providing an unshakable foundation upon which we can rely. In times of weakness, He becomes our source of strength, our savior, and all in all.

God reigns as the ultimate authority, surpassing all others. None can compare to His greatness, and none are more deserving of our adoration. It is solely God who grants us life, triumphing over death and resisting the allure of sin and temptation.

We have countless reasons to extol His virtues, and it is our duty to consistently recognize His magnificence and offer Him the praise He so rightfully merits.

May 18

Isaiah 26:3

When life becomes overwhelming, I find solace in immersing myself in nature. There is an indescribable feeling of rejuvenation that comes from being outdoors, breathing in the crisp air, and being surrounded by the beauty of trees, birds, and sunshine. It's a moment of tranquility that brings me peace.

However, this peacefulness is temporary. So, how can we attain lasting peace throughout the day and night, regardless of our surroundings? This scripture provides a clear answer - by focusing our thoughts on God. It is essential to fill our minds with the teachings of God and firmly stand by them, even when faced with challenges from the world.

It's completely fine to have our own little havens where we can briefly escape from the challenges of life. There's absolutely nothing wrong with finding comfort in a place that refreshes our spirit. However, it's important to remember that true peace can only be found in the Lord, regardless of the circumstances we face.

Let the assurance of God's word give you strength today, even in the midst of the chaos that surrounds you.

May 19

Matthew 6:21

It's natural to enjoy having possessions, but it's important to remember that if you've been fortunate enough to have an abundance, it's essential to share with those in need.

Even if you're not wealthy, using your good health to serve others is a way to contribute to God's Kingdom. By looking out for the needs of others, we are storing up treasures in Heaven that will last for eternity.

In the grand scheme of things, our ultimate goal is to reach Heaven and spend eternity with our beloved Father. All the possessions and worldly treasures we accumulate during our time on Earth will eventually fade away.

None of these materialistic things have any lasting value. However, when we center our attention on Jesus, we lead purposeful lives, concentrating on eternal matters that will never perish.

Let go of all worldly attachments and embrace a life anchored in God. By serving His Kingdom and offering Him honor and praise for the countless blessings bestowed upon us, we can share our abundance with those who are in need.

May 20

John 1:9

Prior to surrendering my life to the Lord, I dwelled in sin and darkness. I relied on false hope in myself and others for salvation, only to end up falling. The only True Light that entered the darkness of this world is Jesus Christ Himself.

The light of Jesus' life shines within us, illuminating our path and dispelling the darkness that surrounds us. This divine transformation, achieved through rebirth and renewal, blesses us with the privilege of being heirs to the Kingdom of Heaven.

Along with this honor comes great responsibility, purpose, and an abundance of blessings that we have been entrusted with.

We who have been saved have experienced the transformative power of Jesus Christ, the True Light. Having been rescued by His grace, we are living proof of His incredible work in our lives and in the lives of those who choose to follow Him wholeheartedly.

As we reflect His light in this dark world, we attract others to Him and bring honor to our Heavenly Father. Jesus is the gift that never stops giving.

May 21

Mark 9:43

It's undeniable that Hell exists, and personally, I have no desire to spend an eternity in such a place. When I made the decision to repent, I realized that there were certain aspects of my life, including certain individuals, that I had to let go of in order to lead a life that truly honored God. I won't deny that it was a challenging journey.

I realized that I had to distance myself from friends struggling with addiction and find a new source of income other than drug dealing. I understood the importance of living in a way that would make God proud to claim me as His own, and in a way that wouldn't lead others astray by my actions.

It's imperative to acknowledge both the grace and wrath of God. Once we have received salvation, our eternal life is assured. However, we must not overlook the fact that God's righteous anger will eventually be unleashed upon this world as a form of judgment, leaving no room for escape for those who have rebelled against Him.

To safeguard ourselves from sin, it is necessary to eliminate any sources of temptation in our lives. Additionally, we should always be prepared to spread the message of salvation, offering others a chance to be saved from the approaching fire.

May 22

Romans 16:20

It is disheartening to witness division within the church and God's family. This division serves as a tool for the enemy to try and tear us apart, and even discourage others from joining the church and God's family.

It is unfortunate that many faithful individuals become targets of such attacks. The devil cunningly manipulates the word of God through those who may not fully comprehend its true meaning or lack a strong foundation in His teachings.

Paul encouraged believers to stay alert in doing good, while also cultivating purity and straightforwardness in dealing with evil. He then promised them that by following these principles, God would ultimately defeat Satan on their behalf.

It's important to stay grounded in the truth of God's word to avoid falling into the devil's traps. Just like how Satan deceived Adam and Eve by twisting God's words, we too can be vulnerable if we're not vigilant.

Do your best to remain steadfast in your faith in order to shield yourself from manipulation. Remember, the path to serving God's Kingdom lies solely in the grace of our faithful Lord Jesus Christ.

May 23

1 Corinthians 13:4-7

It's important to remember that love is a powerful and selfless act that should not be taken lightly. Just like Jesus, who always sought to uplift others even at His own expense, we should strive to show love to everyone, even those who may be difficult to love. By giving love freely, we also open ourselves up to experiencing the awesome love of God.

Our ability to show love and compassion to those who are lost and broken reflects the presence of God in our lives. Take a moment to consider the various aspects of love: being patient, showing kindness, avoiding arrogance and pride, respecting others, not being self-centered, controlling our anger, letting go of past wrongs, rejecting evil and embracing truth, being protective, hopeful, and persistent. These qualities encompass a love that is unwavering and enduring.

It's important for us as followers of Jesus to strive to love like this. Whenever we face challenges, we can turn to our Heavenly Father in prayer for transformation. He has promised to change our hardened hearts into ones filled with love and compassion.

May 24

Jeremiah 17:14

We all experience the need for healing in various aspects of our lives, and there is only one source that can truly restore us: The Lord. At times, His intervention may be miraculous, while other times He may work through individuals like doctors or friends to bring about the healing we seek.

However, it is imperative to remember that He should always be our first point of contact when presenting our requests for healing.

When I was 26 years old, I came close to dying due to endometriosis. The bleeding was so severe that I was on the brink of death before surgery and blood transfusions could save me.

Despite my weakness and fading consciousness, I managed to express my love to my two young children and entrusted my fate to God. Although my faith was not as strong back then, I believed that He was the ultimate decision-maker.

He granted me healing, showing me that His control is absolute, and I understood that healing may sometimes lead to returning to Heaven to be with Him.

It's important to remain faithful, even in the face of death, trusting that His grace will see us through.

May 25

Proverbs 24:32

Reflection can serve as one of life's most valuable teachers. By simply observing the choices and paths taken by those around us, we can gain insight into the consequences of their decisions and the direction it has taken them thus far.

Making wise choices in life has a profound impact on one's journey. It is through these choices that our lives are shaped for the better. On the other hand, when people choose to be lazy and make excuses, life presents them with challenging lessons to learn from.

However, it is important to remember that true success in life comes from embracing God's wisdom and living in reverence of Him. When we do, we pave the way for a fulfilling and prosperous life.

Paying attention to the small details in life and reflecting on their importance can lead us to valuable wisdom and profound insight. By doing so, we can avoid the snares set by the enemy. It allows us to perceive things from a fresh perspective. Seek God's guidance today for wisdom, understanding, and clarity.

Psalms 1:1

If we want to make a difference in this life, it is crucial to have faith in the power of God's word and pray for it to reach every corner of the globe.

By doing so, we can ensure that everyone, regardless of their location, has the chance to experience salvation and embrace the abundant love and blessings of God through Jesus Christ.

It's truly a blessing to have the knowledge of God, especially when others are still searching. If they haven't found Him yet, it means we have a responsibility to guide them towards the right path, as they may be following a different counsel.

Choosing to walk on the path of righteousness is a deliberate decision we make, driven by our deep love and devotion for our savior. It requires immense strength and resilience, as well as surrounding ourselves with individuals who share our beliefs and values.

Evil never rests, so we must remain vigilant against its influence. Let's ensure that we are following God's truth, staying on the right path, and gathering with our fellow believers to learn from Jesus.

May 27

Exodus 20:7

Have you ever wondered what it really means to take the Lord's name in vain? Essentially, it involves lifting up His name in a sinful manner that casts doubt on His reputation. While accepting Jesus Christ as your savior saves you by God's grace, living contrary to His teachings leads to hypocrisy and disrespect towards God.

The significance lies in the reverence we show towards His name. It should be regarded as sacred, not just in our words, but also in the way we, as His children, embody His essence both as individuals and as a collective entity.

When your name is mentioned to someone else, it immediately brings to mind your reputation, which reflects your character and authority. Although misusing God's name will never alter who He is, it can unintentionally or intentionally steer others away from Him.

God emphasizes that it is important to Him how His name is used because His name holds the highest significance, and its misuse can harm relationships with Him. Therefore, we should always show reverence to His name through our words, worship, and actions.

Job 9:10

Our Heavenly Father is incredibly compassionate and generous, surpassing our understanding and imagination. His actions are often hidden from us, working in ways that we cannot fathom.

Throughout our lives, there have been countless instances where He has protected us from disaster or even death, although we may not be aware of them.

Perhaps there were moments when we unintentionally overslept, only to later discover that a terrible accident occurred at the exact time we would have been there. Or maybe we fell ill and missed an event, unknowingly avoiding a tragic incident like a mass shooting.

It is during these times that we realize God's mysterious ways, as what may not initially seem like a blessing is, in fact, a precious gift that saves our lives.

The faithfulness of God is unwavering, His promises remain true. Despite what we see with our eyes, He continuously showers us with His grace in all circumstances. Everything we experience is designed to bring us closer to God and deepen our understanding of His character. May we rely on Him, seek Him, and praise His name.

May 29

1 Corinthians 10:13

During the final stages of my drug addiction, exhaustion consumed me. I was tired of the drugs, the lifestyle, and of myself. Despite feeling this way, I lacked the strength to break free.

One morning, at a friend's house where I was staying, I woke up to find my grandma unexpectedly there, urging me to leave with her. I hesitated, almost giving in, but ultimately chose to remain trapped in my addiction.

As she drove away, I gazed out the open door, sensing that I had just missed my last opportunity to escape that destructive life. Shortly after, I was arrested and spent seven years behind bars. My grandmother was the instrument through which God presented me with an opportunity to escape, yet regrettably, I made the decision not to seize it.

She left me with a nail bent into the form of a heart, attached to a card with a heartfelt poem about the enduring power of love and the opportunity for redemption if we choose to turn away from our sin and embrace a new life through the sacrifice of Jesus Christ.

I still have it to this day, and it continues to remind me of God's unwavering efforts to guide us back to Him, away from the allure of sin and temptation.

May 30

Psalms 139: 23-24

Hidden anxieties have the potential to trap you in a never-ending cycle of worry and fear. Unless you face them head-on with the restorative power of God at their core, they will persistently grow and cause chaos in your life.

It's important to recognize that there is a deeper force at play beyond what we see in the world. Our perception of things is closely tied to the state of our hearts. If our hearts are not aligned with the Lord, our thoughts and attitudes will also be affected.

Similar to David, we should humbly ask the Lord to examine us and guide us away from these negative patterns, towards a path of healing and honoring God.

We must seek God's guidance to discern which viewpoints are in line with His plan. Our limited perspective pales in comparison to His omniscience.

Accepting the truth as it stands demands humility in acknowledging our lack of control, yet finding solace in surrendering our fears, concerns, and stresses to the One who reigns supreme out of His deep love for us, guiding us towards eternal life.

May 31

Isaiah 7:9

It's understandable to feel disheartened or lose hope when faced with challenges in our lives or witnessing turmoil in the world.

However, it's important to remember that Jesus came into this world to remind us that these difficulties are temporary.

Love, an indomitable power, triumphs over every hurdle and remains undefeated. Placing our faith in anything else proves to be fatal for God is Love, and love conquers all.

Jesus Christ is the Way, the Truth, and the Life; there exists no alternative. Neither ourselves nor others, neither wealth nor influence, only Jesus.

The lesson we should take away from this scripture is the importance of wholeheartedly trusting God's word without any hesitation.

He consistently fulfills His promises, and we should not let the distractions of this world shake our faith. Instead, let it motivate us even more to focus on the Lord and keep our gaze fixed upon Him.

June

June 1

Lamentations 3:40

Sometimes it's hard to see the forest because of all the trees. It can be challenging to focus on the bigger picture when we are surrounded by the details of everyday life.

We often become so consumed by our own priorities that we forget to pause and reflect on whether our decisions are in line with what God has intended for us.

We can say that we love God, but the proof is in the pudding so to speak. It's one thing to claim our love for God, but our actions fully reveal the depth of our devotion. Sometimes, we tend to justify our actions to avoid facing the truth and the inner conviction that may disrupt our plans.

To alter our course, it is essential to allocate specific time for introspection, questioning our actions and seeking guidance from both ourselves and God.

Should we discover that we have strayed from the right path, we can seek forgiveness and redirect our journey. Regularly evaluating our choices is vital in order to avoid becoming more lost in the wilderness of life.

June 2

Matthew 5:13

As children of God, it is important for us to understand that just like salt enhances the flavor of a meal, we should strive to enhance the lives of those around us. When people spend time with you, what is the lasting impression they usually walk away with?

When those in our midst observe our journey with the Lord, it should be crystal clear to them that our actions and words are a testament to His goodness.

Our deeds may be the visible manifestation, but it is truly God's divine power at work within us. Let us venture into the frontlines, unafraid to get our hands dirty, and sow the seeds of faith in every corner we tread.

Salt not only adds flavor to our food, but it also plays a key role as a preservative, keeping bacteria at bay and preventing decay. In a similar way, we, as messengers of God, have the power to prevent the spread of sin and death by sharing His word.

Just like salt, if we fail to embrace our purpose and spread our saltiness, the world would rapidly descend into moral decay. Let us continue to be the salt that preserves goodness and righteousness in this world.

June 3

Romans 8:32

It is inherent in our nature as humans to have desires. These desires are personal to each individual and can also serve as a reflection of God’s presence within us.

However, when we prioritize our wants over our longing for a connection with God, these desires can transform into false idols.

God's act of sending His beloved son Jesus Christ to endure a painful death, and a glorious resurrection for our salvation should erase any uncertainty about His willingness to provide us with the greatest blessings life has to offer.

There is no greater gift in this world than the boundless grace that God has given to humanity. As we embrace God's grace through Jesus Christ, we are changed for the better, and our desires start to align with God's purpose for us.

In this alignment, we find that our prayers are answered with a resounding "yes" according to God's perfect will.

Deuteronomy 1:31

Looking back at all the challenges I've faced in life, I can clearly see how God has guided me through each and every one of them.

During times when I was engaging in behaviors that were harmful to me, I now realize that God allowed me to face difficulties in order to redirect my path and open my eyes to a better way.

When I was involved with people who were not meant for me, I can now understand that God allowed those relationships to crumble so that I could find the ones that were indeed meant for me.

And even though I made mistakes and faced spiritual death, God used that moment to grant me a fresh start and bring me to where I am today. It is through His boundless grace, love, and mercy that I am on a journey towards a brighter tomorrow.

Life's challenges may not always feel pleasant, but remember that God is always there to guide and support you through them.

These difficult times are meant to help you grow and strengthen your faith, leading you closer to Him. Just keep in mind that there is always hope and light waiting for you at the end of the tunnel.

June 5

Ruth 2:12

Imagine the sheer beauty and peace of finding refuge as beloved children of the Almighty, nestled beneath the protective embrace of God's wings.

Envision the profound intimacy, where we are shielded with unwavering security and enveloped in boundless love.

But that's not all; this scripture also promises the incredible hope of abundant rewards for every act of goodness we sow on this earthly journey.

The work we undertake for the Kingdom of God possesses significance. He shows concern for us as we carry out the tasks He has assigned to us.

It is important to understand the impact that a single individual, such as yourself, can have.

By immersing yourself in God's word, you can bolster your own abilities and attain satisfaction from serving, understanding that it brings joy to our Heavenly Father who cherishes us and fulfills all our needs.

June 6

Proverbs 4:23

Your life is a reflection of what fills your heart. In this passage, the heart symbolizes your emotions, thoughts, will, and deepest being. The state of your heart serves as a spiritual barometer, revealing the overall well-being of your life.

The heart is like the control center for all our life decisions. It's important to keep it healthy because everything we do stems from it. Just like we'd see a doctor for a physical heart issue, we should turn to the Lord for spiritual heart problems. By filling our hearts with Him, we can ensure that our actions are pure and good.

Taking care of your heart involves nourishing it with good things to ensure its optimal functioning. It's similar to the contrast between consuming a nutritious diet versus indulging in a diet packed with sugar, grease, carbs, fat, and caffeine.

Unhealthy eating habits gradually weaken our bodies, leading to signs of decline or even death if not addressed. Conversely, maintaining a healthy diet offers the advantage of a longer and better-quality life.

Our spiritual nourishment works in a similar way. God has graciously provided us with the Bread of Life, but it's up to you to partake of its goodness.

June 7

Lamentations 3:22-23

The rising of the sun brings forth a glimmer of promise, a ray of hope that fills our hearts with anticipation.

As the sun's gentle beams illuminate the world, they serve as a reminder of God's unwavering faithfulness.

In the face of our current challenges, tomorrow holds the potential for a fresh start, a chance to overcome the falsehoods of hopelessness and the weight of despair.

Through Jesus Christ, our devoted Father has bestowed upon us a living hope, a beacon of light that guides us through the darkness of this world, ensuring that it never consumes us completely.

The Lord understands our sorrow and is always near to provide comfort. During these moments, we can depend on His power and have faith in His new mercies every morning.

God will come to you wherever you may be. Raise your heart and hands to your Heavenly Father, worship and call upon His name, and He will give you His peace beyond understanding along with His unfailing love.

June 8

John 15:18

When we decide to walk the path of our Savior Jesus Christ, it's important to realize that we will inevitably encounter challenges similar to the ones He faced.

The truth is often unwelcome in the world, as it tries to silence it by any means necessary. Due to sin, those who believe will experience opposition and alienation from non-believers.

Jesus shared this scripture as a cautionary message to help us strengthen our faith in times of adversity.

In these difficult times, it is important for us to follow the example of Jesus. We should strive to maintain inner peace and not let resentment consume us.

It is no surprise if the world opposes us, but we can be ready by immersing ourselves in God's teachings.

Jesus never imposed His beliefs on others; He simply fulfilled His purpose, and those who were open to the truth accepted Him with humility and gratitude.

June 9

Romans 8:38-39

These two verses are a powerful reminder of the immense love that God has for you. There is absolutely nothing that can hinder His love for us. God remains steadfast in His love, even when we may turn away from Him.

His love for us knows no bounds and is unwavering. He is a faithful Husband, always loving us, even when we may be unfaithful.

When I was living in sin, I vividly recall questioning the whereabouts of God amidst the chaos and turmoil I was experiencing. Little did I realize, He was by my side the entire time, urging me to change my ways and return to His loving embrace.

Instead of questioning God's presence, I should have reflected on where I stood within the vastness of His love. I continuously placed myself in questionable situations and then became resentful towards God for not fulfilling my desires.

It was not His love that faltered, but rather my own shortcomings. Nevertheless, even in those moments, He fought for me relentlessly.

The love He has for us is unshakeable, and nothing can ever come between us and that love.

June 10

Psalms 25:4

We all make mistakes, and it's important to remember that God understands this. He hopes that we will learn from our mistakes and move forward. This means admitting when we've messed up and making a conscious effort to avoid repeating those same mistakes.

In order to grow, we need to remain open to learning and luckily, we have the best teacher available to us - God. Seeking wisdom is the first step, and God is more than willing to grant us this gift when we ask for it.

We have the Holy Spirit within us to guide and correct us, but it's essential that we humble ourselves and bring our concerns to God. We must then patiently wait for His response and be willing to obediently follow His guidance.

God is not only our teacher but also our guide. When we approach Him with reverence, He will never leave us feeling lost in the darkness. He is our loving Savior, always ready to lead us towards everlasting life.

Approach each new day with a receptive and eager heart, seeking chances to listen to His guidance as you walk in His mercy and grace.

June 11

Isaiah 2:22

Have you ever tallied up the number of times you've been disappointed by someone? It could have been a close friend you trusted. Or a relative who wasn't there for you in your time of need. Perhaps it was your partner who let you down. Or maybe, it was even yourself.

The bottom line is, we all make mistakes. The only one we can truly rely on is the Almighty. We shouldn't let human shortcomings cloud our faith in God's reliability. We need to have faith in Him above all else.

We can't predict what tomorrow holds, but we know the one who holds tomorrow in His hands. The person we rely on today may not be there tomorrow, and the same goes for ourselves.

Every day, we place our trust in various people, whether it's the hairdresser who styles our hair or the doctor who prescribes our medication. However, it's important to remember that they too are human and prone to making mistakes. While people strive to do their best, sometimes their efforts fall short.

In such moments, it is comforting to know that God is the ultimate authority. He has the power to bring all things together for our ultimate good.

June 12

Luke 16:13

Jesus cautions us about the impossibility of serving both money and God simultaneously. If our primary goal revolves around accumulating material wealth, then money undeniably becomes our ruler.

However, if we make conscious decisions guided by God's will, then He becomes our ultimate authority. God longs for our wholehearted devotion, and there is only room for one object of our affection.

We cannot go right and left at the same time; we must choose a direction. Furthermore, God never imposes Himself upon us; He grants us the free will to steer our own lives.

In an instant, all material riches can vanish into thin air. Economic downturns, unforeseen health problems, or even a devastating tornado can wipe out your financial assets and cherished possessions.

But God's presence is eternal, and so are the everlasting treasures He has prepared for you in Heaven.

June 13

Romans 1:12

During my seven years of incarceration, being separated from my family was hard. However, the women I lived with all those years became my new family and support system.

We leaned on each other, shared our faith, and stood together through thick and thin. Our bond in Jesus Christ shone brightly, even within the prison walls. Our kindness and faith drew others to seek guidance and prayer from us.

It taught me that God's light can never be dimmed by darkness, and that love knows no bounds, even in unexpected places. Our mutual encouragement of faith not only made our time in prison more bearable, but also deepened our connection with God, leading others to Him.

Facing trials and challenges in life is inevitable, but we are not alone. God is our ultimate support, and He also surrounds us with a community of believers who embody His love and care.

Sometimes, we may even find that support is within ourselves to offer others.

June 14

2 Corinthians 12:9-10

After enduring many tumultuous years with my first spouse on and off, battling addiction for three challenging years following our separation, and spending seven years behind bars, I witnessed the incredible transformation that the Lord brought upon me and my life through these trials.

As a result, the very first thing I did was use my voice to proudly boast of my weaknesses. I eagerly share with anyone who is willing to lend an ear about the extraordinary miracles that God performed within me and all around me.

People used to believe that I would never change or that I would meet a tragic end. However, if you were to meet me today without any knowledge of my past, you would never suspect the darkness I once lived through. All of this is solely the work of God.

I regret some decisions I made in the past, yet I am unashamed to share how God provided me with His strength and rescued me. Despite facing opposition, I firmly believe that God deserves to be praised and acknowledged.

Sharing your vulnerabilities with others requires immense strength and bravery, yet you can always rely on the Lord's strength to guide you through.

June 15

Galatians 2:20

When we experience rebirth, it signifies that we have let go of all the things that once held us captive, allowing us to flourish in service to God.

Our continuous transformation is aimed at reflecting the likeness of Christ. Each of us has encountered a personal connection with Him, which has strengthened our faith as the Holy Spirit leads us and connects us to our Creator.

As we navigate through our daily lives, we may encounter numerous faces, but my deepest desire is for others to see the face of Jesus when they see us, above all else.

All the acts of love we perform are a reflection of our faith in Jesus. The lives we live now are no longer ours to control, but now belong to the Savior who sacrificed His own life for us.

Through this surrender, we can find fulfillment and joy in serving others. By being united with Christ, we embody His teachings and values. Just as Jesus triumphed over death, we too have been reborn, and it is in this resurrection that we discover our true selves.

June 16

Romans 8:31

Challenges are inevitable in life, but it's how we tackle them that really matters. While God is always on our side, it doesn't guarantee that everything will go our way.

However, we can find comfort in knowing that if something is truly meant for us according to God's plan, nothing can prevent us from achieving it. And if it's not meant for us, we can trust that God will guide us towards what is.

While some things may effortlessly fall into place, others require dedication, persistence, and unwavering faith. These are the experiences that shape us, molding us into stronger believers.

They are like spiritual workouts, building our resilience and character. And when we finally reach our desired destination, the taste of victory becomes even more satisfying.

Focus on the one who can move mountains instead of dwelling on the mountain itself. Remember, the challenges you're facing right now won't last forever. Trust in God's guidance and you'll find the strength to overcome any fear.

Psalms 19:13

It can be difficult to resist the temptation to commit sin, but it's important to remember that all sin is a way of turning away from God.

This passage highlights the seriousness of deliberate sin, when we knowingly choose to do wrong despite understanding the consequences.

Before I embraced Jesus as my savior, my life was consumed by addiction and filled with regrettable decisions. At that time, I didn't fully grasp the magnitude of my wrongdoing and the repercussions that awaited me.

However, once I repented and surrendered my life to Jesus, I understood that reverting to my previous lifestyle would mean facing God's judgment, knowing that I had knowingly turned away from Him.

It would be a deliberate and conscious choice to abandon God and return to my former sinful ways. Thankfully, we have the ability to rely on God's strength to walk in His grace and strive to live a blameless life.

June 18

Daniel 9:18-19

As we watch the news and witness the increasing prevalence of sin in the world, along with a concerning number of individuals who have grown complacent towards it, it is crucial for us to intercede for our fellow believers in prayer.

We can confess the sins we witness to God and earnestly implore Him to listen to our prayers and take action. Additionally, we should humbly acknowledge our own transgressions and genuinely repent.

We understand that we are unworthy of God's grace and forgiveness, but we can trust in His faithfulness to protect what is rightfully His. Just like Daniel approached God, beseeching Him to intervene because His city and people needed Him, we too have the opportunity to bring our concerns to God.

Rest assured that our heartfelt prayers will resound with utmost clarity to our Heavenly Father. When we beseech God to manifest His glory, we can be certain that He will answer the call for all those who bear His name. Remember, you are deeply cherished and valued as His beloved sons and daughters.

Matthew 24:44

It can be quite unsettling when someone unexpectedly shows up at your door, especially at an inopportune time. You may not have been ready for a surprise visitor.

Perhaps you were still in your pajamas, or your home was a mess, leaving you feeling a bit embarrassed about the situation. This is similar to what the day will be like when our Lord Jesus Christ returns.

It's important to keep your spiritual house in order, rather than procrastinating and being caught off guard. By staying connected to God's word, surrounding yourself with fellow believers, sharing the gospel, and living according to God's plan, you can ensure that you are spiritually prepared.

It's similar to waking up early to clean the house and prepare yourself, just in case an unexpected guest pays a visit. Those who are well-prepared will be richly rewarded as dedicated servants who stayed watchful and attentive.

June 20

1 Corinthians 3:16

Understanding the concept of the Holy Spirit dwelling within you can be a profound experience. It signifies a transformation within, a shift towards a life guided by God's presence.

The power of the Holy Spirit manifests in various ways, such as speaking God's word boldly and reflecting His image in our daily lives.

This indwelling Spirit serves as a seal of our belonging to God, a promise of our inheritance, and a guarantee of our future glory in Heaven.

This sacred connection you have the privilege of sharing with God is a lifelong journey of intimacy. It is a divine partnership that should inspire you to strive for greater holiness.

Remember, the same Spirit that resurrected Jesus is the very power residing inside of you. Embrace this divine presence within you and let it guide you on your spiritual journey.

June 21

Exodus 20:15

When someone engages in theft, it signifies multiple underlying factors. Firstly, it indicates a violation of God's teachings and a rebellious act against His word.

Moreover, it reflects a lack of love towards one's neighbor, as no one desires to have their possessions stolen. However, it also reveals a lack of faith in the Lord's ability to provide for one's needs.

Stealing can take various forms, such as failing to use one's talents and gifts to serve God's Kingdom, withholding earnings by not tithing, or even directly stealing someone's property.

Theft also includes deceptive tactics aimed at gaining financial advantage, misappropriating funds or assets, or taking something without the person's consent because they were not fully informed.

God's ultimate desire is for us to fulfill our responsibilities, embrace honesty, and treat others with the same love and respect that we yearn for. God is ever ready to meet all our needs.

June 22

Psalms 37:9

It's not uncommon to feel frustrated when we see the wicked prospering while we struggle. However, the key is not to question God's greatness, but to shift our focus onto ourselves.

The truth is, those who prosper in this life will only enjoy their glory temporarily. The treasures they accumulate will not last forever. God has made it clear that the wicked will eventually be destroyed.

On the other hand, those of us who patiently wait for the Lord will inherit what is rightfully ours. As we break free from generational sin and face challenges, our spiritual strength will be tested.

But the things we build through God's righteousness will lead to prosperity and stability. It's essential for us to stay focused on God's word and promises, to hold onto our faith and hope in the Lord, and to never give up.

Entrust your cares, hopes, desires, worries, and frustrations to God. Draw your attention to the one who loves you instead of everything happening around you. Allow Him to be your quiet place among the storms of life.

June 23

Matthew 19:26

We cannot purchase our entrance into Heaven or earn our place in God's Kingdom through good deeds or hard work. Salvation is only attainable through Jesus Christ and God's grace. The Lord is our sole source of hope for salvation. It is not about our actions, but rather what God has already accomplished for us.

We have no need to prove ourselves because Jesus has already accomplished everything on our behalf. Our only task is to accept Him as the ruler of our lives. This verse emphasizes God's omnipotence, His complete authority to act as He pleases.

However, it does not imply that we will always have our desires fulfilled simply because we have God in our lives. Instead, it signifies that all things are possible according to His will, which aligns with His ultimate plan.

The context of this passage revolves around the topic of salvation, which should be approached humbly by fully trusting in our faithful Savior. We must yield to His plan, knowing He will bring about what is best for us, even if it means not getting our way. If everyone always had their desires fulfilled, the world would descend into chaos and catastrophe.

June 24

John 16:20

I recall the shocking moment my brother passed away at the age of 38 due to a drug overdose. He worked as a Millwright, traveled extensively, earned a good income, and seemed to be enjoying life. However, he had been battling depression and addiction on and off for years. We were unaware that he had relapsed.

Once the funeral service concluded, the full force of grief hit me like a tidal wave. I doubted my ability to cope on my own, and indeed, I couldn't. After months of struggling with my sorrow, I made the decision to surrender it to God.

I made a conscious effort to thank God daily for the happy memories I shared with my brother and for the time we spent together. I took control of my thoughts, redirecting them towards praise and gratitude to God for His blessings, reminding myself that the Lord gives, and the Lord takes away.

God used this painful experience to work through me, allowing me to help save lives by mentoring addicts and incarcerated individuals. Now, when I think of my brother, his memory fills my heart with love and gratitude, knowing that his legacy is making a positive impact on others.

June 25

Romans 12:6

It was a challenging journey for me when I was reborn, not knowing how God would use me in His Kingdom. Discovering my purpose and gifts felt like starting from scratch, like learning to walk all over again.

Everything seemed unfamiliar. I had only known my old ways, which no longer served me. So, I turned to God in prayer, seeking guidance. Eventually, I found a Christian community and surrounded myself with like-minded individuals. I felt a strong calling to minister to addicts, those behind bars, and to write Christian books.

God kept orchestrating encounters with people in need, leading me to where I needed to be. Many encouraged me to write a book, and one day, I heeded God's call in my life. The rest, as they say, is history. Each of us has unique gifts given to us through our life experiences, and God will place us where we can use them to bring glory to Him.

As you continue on your journey and actively use your spiritual gifts, they will undoubtedly grow stronger. It's natural to stumble a bit at first, but don't lose heart. Stay committed and watch how God glorifies you as you glorify Him.

June 26

Haggai 1:5-6

The world may not want to hear this particular scripture, but it serves as a wake-up call from God for us to reflect on our actions.

It's a reminder to confront our own flaws, especially our tendencies towards selfishness and greed. Choosing to acknowledge our wrongdoings and then continuing to live in sin is essentially turning our backs on God.

When we are blessed with abundance, it's meant for us to use in service of His Kingdom, not to squander on every selfish desire. God wants us to sow seeds of kindness and nurture the growth of goodness in others we encounter.

Let's always remember the true source of our blessings and the purpose behind them. By prioritizing the Kingdom of God, everything else will fall into place according to His divine plan.

Our compassionate Father has showered us with countless blessings and expects very little in return. Moreover, whatever He does request from us, He equips us with the necessary resources to fulfill it. All He asks is that we play our role with gratitude, relying on His mercy and grace.

Job 6:8

At times, life can give us the impression that God is against us. It may seem like everything around us is crumbling and falling apart, and there may have been moments when we pleaded with God to end our suffering because it became unbearable.

Job experienced this very feeling because he couldn't comprehend God's greater plan. He endured immense suffering, and his supposed friends offered no support to uplift him.

Throughout the Bible, there are numerous instances where people question whether the Lord is with them and on their side. However, the truth remains that God is always by our side and always in our favor. It's possible that we may not fully grasp His plan in the present moment, but if we hold on, persevere, and maintain our faith, we will eventually reach the other side - the promised land where we will witness His blessings.

We were never guaranteed an easy life or that we would obtain everything we desire. The only assurance we were given is that we will face troubles, but we should take solace in the fact that Jesus has overcome them.

2 Chronicles 14:11

The notion of something being impossible is a human construct. The Lord does not recognize the concept of impossibility. When confronted with challenging circumstances, we limit our perception of God if we try to convince ourselves that there is no way forward.

God has a track record of accomplishing the unimaginable. He has resurrected the dead, provided a path where there seemed to be none through Jesus Christ, miraculously fed multitudes with meager provisions, brought down rulers and kingdoms that opposed Him, and used a young man armed with only a stone to defeat a formidable giant warrior.

The magnificence, love, and might of our God are beyond comprehension. Therefore, when you find yourself facing your own version of an overwhelming force, remember who your God is and that you bear His name, knowing that He will never allow His name to be defeated.

You may have to endure a period of hardship, but ultimately God will bring about victory for Himself through your circumstances.

Genesis 3:4

Satan's ultimate objective is to create a significant gap between you and God. His aim is to divert your attention, overwhelm you, and make you focus on anything and everything except God.

He wants to confuse you and make you believe that God is not on your side, that He is indifferent and unsympathetic towards your circumstances.

Satan would be delighted if you blamed God for all the negativity in the world. He wants you to question and doubt everything that your loving Father has communicated to you.

You must remain consistently rooted in the truth, otherwise, you will easily be led astray. God has provided us with His word to study and share with others, so that we are aware of the boundaries He has set for us on our life's journey.

Satan and his army are relentless and will continuously test your boundaries for weaknesses. We must rely on our divine discernment to determine whether the things presented to us are from God or if they are traps set by the enemy.

1 Samuel 25:6

The power of words is undeniable, especially when we are guided by the Holy Spirit. With the Holy Spirit working within us, we possess a formidable weapon to combat the forces of darkness.

Through our words, we have the ability to speak blessings and bring life to others, their families, their careers, and their futures. It is not limited to just those who are close to us; we should also extend these words of positivity to our enemies.

Every victory for the Kingdom of God is a defeat for the devil. Our focus should be on saving souls rather than condemning them.

This verse emphasizes the significance of peace, kindness, and a deep love for God above all else, even in the midst of conflict or persecution.

It can be challenging when others don't treat us well, but we have the power to let God's Spirit shine His righteousness through us by maintaining a sincere heart of peace, especially during tough times.

July

July 1

Proverbs 19:21

I can still recall the day I met my first husband. We were teenagers and fell head over heels in love in no time. Everything happened so quickly - he moved in with me within a month and we tied the knot shortly after.

Looking back, it was evident that God was trying to show us that we were not meant to be together. Unfortunately, we were too young and inexperienced to realize that, and our emotions often got the best of us.

Our relationship was a rollercoaster of chaos and instability. We made plans, but nothing ever seemed to work out. The root of the issue was that we failed to seek God's guidance before making decisions to see if it was part of His plan too.

It took many years to understand this, but eventually, the Lord led me to the person I was truly meant to be with. Now, instead of things falling apart, we have built a strong foundation together.

We communicate effectively, enjoy each other's company, and are excited about growing old together. We also bring our hopes and dreams before the Lord, ensuring that they are aligned with God's plans before moving forward.

July 2

Isaiah 9:2

God sent Jesus into the world as a symbol of hope, a radiant light amidst the darkness to guide us when we are lost. Regrettably, there will always be those who prefer the darkness over the light.

However, those who embrace the light of truth and life will be rewarded with glory. Living in the light may not always be comfortable, as it exposes what was once concealed by darkness. We must be willing to confront the darkness within us and allow the light to drive it away.

Our human nature is naturally inclined towards sin and selfish desires as we were once spiritually dead due to our transgressions. Once we choose to dwell in the light, we engage in a battle against our fleshly desires as our new Heavenly nature clashes with our sinful nature.

With the help of the Holy Spirit, the guidance of Jesus Christ, and the teachings of God's word, we experience a newfound life and triumph like never before. This light begins to radiate from our hearts, influencing the world around us and drawing us closer to our Lord and the eternal glory that awaits us.

July 3

Luke 16:10

Faithfulness holds great importance in the eyes of God. He blesses us in a way that reveals our true relationship with Him, examining whether we will prioritize ourselves or honor Him with the blessings He provides. How we act when we have very little speaks volumes about our character and what we would do if given more.

My wise great grandma used to say, "Believe someone's true colors the first time they show them to you!" And she couldn't have been more right. If you were to hire an employee and discovered they were stealing small amounts of money, you certainly wouldn't want to promote them to a position where they handle your bank deposits. The way we handle the little we have reflects our willingness to serve the Kingdom of God through faith.

The abundance that awaits us is directly linked to how we honor our Heavenly Father with what little we possess. Every decision we make holds immense significance to God. He desires that His blessings are not squandered by our selfish appetites. Through God's grace, we can learn to love and serve others, trusting that He will always provide for our needs.

July 4

Romans 12:2

Breaking free from the chains of sin and experiencing a complete transformation of the mind is the ultimate freedom. It's how we align ourselves with our loving Creator and Savior, with the guidance of the Holy Spirit.

Although we may still reside in this world, we no longer belong to it. Our true home is in Heaven, and this earthly existence is just a temporary passing through.

The journey of transformation is a beautiful adventure fueled by love. We understand that it begins by immersing ourselves in the word of God, whether it's through listening, reading, or applying it in our lives.

It's important to make time every day to connect with God's word in order to refresh our minds. This can be done through reading the Bible, going to church, joining an online program, or taking part in a Bible study group.

Transformation doesn't happen overnight; it requires a conscious and continuous effort. Remember, what we fill our minds with shapes who we become. So, let go of the past and allow God to usher in a new chapter in your life!

Micah 7:7

When I shared my testimony of how God saved me through His grace, I received an outpouring of positive responses and support. However, there were also those who didn't believe in God and mocked Him or felt I shouldn't share my personal journey so openly.

It took a lot of courage to speak about the details of my salvation, and I had to learn not to take negative reactions personally. I responded with grace and kindness, or sometimes chose not to respond at all.

Even now, I still receive messages from people with different beliefs, but my personal encounter with God is unshakeable. I know He is as real as the air I breathe, and I will continue to worship Him faithfully.

I patiently (and sometimes impatiently) await His return, knowing He loves me, hears my prayers, and is waiting to welcome me with open arms in Heaven.

July 6

Isaiah 1:19

When I was living in sin, I experienced great loss. I lost my job, home, family members, and even friends. There were even days when I went without food.

Despite all of this, God continued to love me and provide for my needs. It was my own unwillingness to turn away from my sinful ways and my disobedience that prevented me from living in the blessings that God had intended for me.

It's important to remember that we cannot earn God's grace or blessings through our actions, but we can open ourselves up to receiving the blessings that are meant for us. My sinful behavior was essentially blocking the goodness that was meant to come into my life.

Now that I have a willing heart and strive to be obedient, I have found stability in my home, a loving husband, healthy relationships, a pantry filled with food, and so much more. God's goodness is always within reach for all of us, we just need to take that first step and walk in His direction.

Joshua 24:15

Choosing a side and standing firm on it is pivotal when it comes to your belief system. Straddling the fence won't last long. You can't have it both ways, being hot and cold simultaneously.

The world constantly bombards us with temptations, urging us to worship its idols like sex, money, and technology. It's easy to get caught up in the allure of pleasure, fame, power, and instant gratification. If we prioritize these things above all else, we're definitely on the wrong side of the fence.

This decision, my dear, is the most important one you'll ever make. And guess what? You have to make it every single day, repeatedly. It's a call to serve and a summons to choose.

Our devotion to God must be genuine, and from the heart. Always keep in mind that the choices you make will impact both your life on Earth and your eternal destination. So, make your decisions wisely, my friend.

July 8

Psalms 18:28

We all experience challenging times in life. There are moments that are difficult to handle. We have a choice to trust in God during these times or to feel upset because things are not going as we hoped. These moments can make us feel very alone.

I recall the time when my stepdad visited me in prison shortly before my release. He shared with me that he had terminal cancer and only had about three months to live. My main concern was his salvation. He had not yet embraced Jesus, and I was determined to help him do so before it was too late.

I began praying for him, sent him scriptures, and the salvation prayer. One day, I called him, and he said he had read the salvation prayer I sent, and accepted Jesus Christ as his Lord and Savior! It was nothing short of a miracle.

I laid my hands on him the next time I saw him, prayed for his healing, and asked God to send His angels to protect him. It has been over four years since that moment, and his cancer is no longer detectable on his scans. When you are faced with darkness, remember the one who can bring light and life into every situation.

July 9

Mark 7:15

Social media has become dominant in this era. Undeniably, it offers numerous advantages as an excellent platform for business promotion and enables us to stay connected with distant family members and friends.

However, it also has its drawbacks. It can be deceptive. As we browse through people's posts, we often witness them appearing happy and seemingly free from problems, living their best lives. Yet, if we were to delve deeper, the reality would not be as picture-perfect.

This analogy can be applied to our spiritual lives as well. We may put on a facade, attempting to convince the world that our lives are flawless and virtuous, and we may even succeed in doing so, but God sees and comprehends the true state of our hearts.

Sooner or later, this truth will become evident in our everyday lives, and the entire world will see it for what it is. Putting on a facade takes a lot of work, which is why the first step towards living your most fulfilling life is to look within and let the light of God cleanse and work through you.

July 10

1 Corinthians 3:9

We are the soil in which the gospel was planted. The soil requires constant care, and fortunately, God is a meticulous gardener who pays attention to every detail.

We are also living temples of the Lord, and together we form a building, the true church. This church is not a building made of bricks or stone, but rather it is us.

God nurtures the seed planted within us until we resemble our Lord Jesus Christ. Although God doesn't need us, He graciously offers us the honor and privilege of being ambassadors of Christ, equipping each of us with unique gifts to serve the Kingdom of God.

Remember, you are not alone on this journey. God Himself and your fellow brothers and sisters in Christ are fighting alongside you, triumphantly pushing back the forces of darkness.

Embrace your individuality as you serve the Lord. We are like different puzzle pieces, skillfully arranged by God's hand to create a beautiful picture together!

July 11

Ecclesiastes 7:14

When everything is going smoothly in life, it's easy to attribute it to God's love, blessings, and favor.

However, when life takes a turn and becomes challenging, we often question whether God is still present and caring for us. The truth is, it's not about God's love for us, but rather our perspective.

God's love for us is unwavering and infinite. These difficult chapters in our lives are often the very things that shape us and prepare us for the blessings that lie ahead.

They have a way of refining us and purging the negativity we've been holding onto. It's God's way of cleaning house, making room for new beginnings.

How many times have you looked back on your life and recalled the blessings that emerged from the burdens?

Remember, nothing is impossible for the Lord. He will guide you through every mountain and valley you encounter. Trust in His love and His plan for you.

July 12

Proverbs 20:22

In my thirties, my boyfriend broke into my house and shattered both of my wrists. I vividly remember the mix of satisfaction and fear on his face as I lay on the ground, pleading for help.

The doctors and nurses put me back together, but I was left with casts up to my shoulders as I left the hospital. I wanted justice, feeling hurt and angry. He had never laid a hand on me before, catching me completely off guard.

When he cruelly mocked my temporary disability via text, I prayed for divine retribution. It took time, but he was eventually arrested, tried, and sentenced to prison.

God delivered justice, albeit not in the way or timeframe I expected. Shortly after, he was in a serious car accident, leaving him temporarily disabled. God not only vindicated me, but also made him understand the challenges of being impaired.

Today, my ex is a fellow brother in Christ, happily married, saved by grace, and dedicated to serving the Lord and his family. Trust the process, for God's plan is always at work.

1 Kings 8:30

Our Heavenly Father longs to hear from us. There is no need for uncertainty, as He has graciously sent His one and only son, Jesus Christ, to pave the way for us to communicate with Him and be united with Him for eternity after this life.

The location of your prayers is insignificant; what simply matters is that you pray. Whether you pray in a church, your bedroom, amidst nature, or in the shower, God will listen to you. Prayer should be a sincere expression from your heart, connecting with God's.

God is faithful and attentive to our prayers. He is the focal point where we should bring all our worries and praises. When you come to Him with a humble and repentant heart, He will not only listen to your prayers but also offer forgiveness.

You are cherished by Him; you are the precious gem His heart eagerly awaits. Take a moment today to reflect on how significant you are to God and express gratitude for the love He showers upon your life.

July 14

1 Samuel 12:24

There is a motto that many people follow that says, "live like there's no tomorrow!" However, I choose to live differently. I believe in living a life that considers the consequences of today for tomorrow.

Living recklessly without thinking about the future can lead to risky behaviors and facing the consequences later on. Every day, I strive to ask myself, "How can I honor the Lord in this situation?"

He has blessed me abundantly and helped me through challenges I never imagined overcoming. Therefore, I prioritize honoring Him over my own selfish desires the best that I can.

It's not always easy, as there are moments when I feel angry or lazy, but I remember how God has always been there for me, offering grace instead of judgment.

This motivates me to become a better person each day. I may not be perfect, but I strive for improvement and face each day with gratitude and humility towards God.

July 15

Psalms 27:4

I long to be enveloped in God's grace and to cultivate a deeper, more meaningful connection with Him. There are days when I seek solace in His presence, overwhelmed by the challenges of the world, craving His peace, love, provision, affection, and protection.

And then there are moments when I simply want to bask in the wonder of His existence, finding comfort in the rock of my salvation. God has been by our side in the past, is here with you in this moment, and will continue to be with you every step of the way.

He is the beauty that emerges from the ashes within the sacred temple that is your soul. If there is one thing I wish for you in life, it is to invite Jesus into your heart as your Lord and Savior. This single request encompasses all you could ever need and desire.

May you never forget that you are a beloved child of God, cherished beyond measure and destined for glory.

July 16

Matthew 18:20

We are well aware that God's presence is constant, whether we find ourselves alone or surrounded by a multitude of fellow believers. This passage specifically emphasizes God's presence when we pray for and correct a brother or sister in Christ who has strayed from the right path.

It is our duty to approach them with love and offer assistance in finding their way back. If our initial efforts fail, we should seek guidance from more experienced members of our church. And if that doesn't yield results, we must surrender the situation to the Lord through prayer.

As a church, we understand that God is always with us, supporting us and desiring that none should be lost. He will stand with us as we remain steadfast in His righteous teachings.

It is crucial for us to put aside our differences and allow the Holy Spirit to work through us, leading others back to God.

Malachi 3:6-7

There is a single path to return to the Lord when we falter, and that is to admit our sins, repent, and follow God's guidance in our lives. We are fortunate to have a God who remains constant and loves us unconditionally, regardless of how far we may have strayed.

His response is always a resounding yes when we seek His forgiveness and turn away from our sinful ways. Because God is unwavering, we have the opportunity to approach Him with respect and choose Him over destruction.

As long as we are alive, we have the freedom to walk on the bridge that is Jesus Christ and into the embrace of our loving Father. God constructed the bridge, but it is our responsibility to cross it.

Our final destination is determined by the choices we make using the gift of free will that the Lord has graciously given us. Trusting in God's plan may be daunting at times, but the promise of glory far surpasses what awaits us in the opposite direction.

July 18

Romans 8:17

The narrative of Jesus Christ represents both a tragic tale and an extraordinary demonstration of overcoming life's challenges. It embodies courage, self-discipline, grace, selflessness, love, sorrow, and triumph.

Jesus endured immense suffering, to the point of sweating blood. He came to live as a human being, providing us with an example of how to respond under the most agonizing circumstances.

He also came to show us what awaits us if we follow in His footsteps. No one will ever suffer more than He did, and no one will ever be more glorified than He. Out of love for His Father and for us, He took upon Himself the sins of the world, which moves me to tears every time I contemplate it.

Therefore, we must acknowledge that we will also partake in His sufferings as we live our own human experience, but we can be certain that all is not lost and that our sufferings are not without purpose. As we share in His sufferings, we will also be lifted up to share in His eternal glory.

July 19

Genesis 1:3

Words have the power to build up or tear down, to inspire or discourage, to heal or harm. They have the ability to create and destroy, to bring joy or sorrow. Our words have the power to shape our reality and the reality of those around us.

When we speak words of love, encouragement, and positivity, we are inviting blessings and abundance into our lives. Conversely, when we speak words of hate, criticism, and negativity, we are inviting destruction and chaos.

It is important to be mindful of the words we speak, as they have the power to create our reality. By speaking words of faith, hope, and love, we can align ourselves with God's will and bring about positive change in our lives and the lives of others.

Let us remember the power of spoken words and use them wisely, for they have the ability to shape our world and bring about transformation. Let us speak life into existence and watch as miracles unfold before our eyes.

July 20

Luke 7:47

People often ask me, "How do you manage to have compassion and empathy for rapists, murderers, addicts, and thieves?" My response is simple: it's because Jesus has a heart for them, and when I found Jesus, He gave me His heart.

Because Jesus forgave me, I am able to love unconditionally. I firmly believe that no one is beyond redemption, as I myself was once considered a lost cause.

We must stop judging with our human hearts and start embodying the image of Jesus Christ. We are called to lead these individuals out of darkness and into the light.

We are the laborers in God's field, tasked with bringing about change. We must rise above our own understanding and fulfill the work the Lord has called us to do.

Let us remember the countless times Jesus never turned His back on us and be grateful for His unfailing love.

July 21

Mark 5:34

The power conveyed in this passage is remarkable. It highlights the transformative power of having faith in Jesus.

The woman in this scripture was healed because she approached Jesus with unwavering faith, fully believing that she would be healed. Despite the large crowd, she persevered, and Jesus took notice of her faith.

She understood that He was the only solution. Jesus has the ability to turn any situation around, but we must actively seek Him out, no matter the obstacles, and have faith that He will heal our situation according to His plan.

Jesus loves us unconditionally, regardless of our physical or emotional state. He desires to bring healing to us and urges us to seek Him out, knowing that He is the Way, the Truth, and the Life, and is ready to welcome us.

He also encourages us to express gratitude for the blessings He bestows upon us and to fully embrace every moment of life.

Acts 20:24

Jesus has entrusted us with a mission - to spread the good news! Sharing the gospel can be done in various ways, and one impactful method is by sharing your personal journey of faith.

Every time you open up about your experiences, you are linking your life to the eternal truth found in God's word and the promises He has fulfilled in your life.

By sharing the good news, barriers are broken, wounds are healed, and connections are made, allowing God's light to shine through and illuminate the darkest corners.

Reflecting on the challenges you have faced and how you have triumphed through God's grace is a wonderful way to reclaim your power!

Some days may feel overwhelmingly heavy, while others may feel light and easy, but each day is a gift with its own unique blessings.

Never give up! And never allow the devil to steal your voice. With God by your side, there is no need to fear.

Romans 1:16

Sadly, there are those who are unaware or unwilling to acknowledge the beauty of salvation through Jesus Christ. I remember the time when I initially launched a social media page to share my books, blogs, and anything that I believed brought glory to God.

About 90% of the time, I received positive feedback, but the remaining 10% could be quite unpleasant. I found myself praying for these people because they were lost and filled with anger.

It brought me comfort to know that Jesus too faced similar challenges and did not allow it to hinder Him from spreading His message. I never responded with anger or judgmental words, I simply entrusted it to God, but I never allowed anyone's unkindness or cruelty to weaken my faith or my purpose. If anything, it only motivated me to persevere even more and speak up even louder.

Once I recognized God's presence in my life, there was no turning back. I am proud to be His daughter and a part of His church, which is His bride. There will always be those who oppose you and test your faith, but we can always respond with love and remain steadfast on the foundation that is Jesus Christ.

July 24

Joel 2:32

We are reminded that no matter how difficult life may become, we are not alone. Jesus Christ is our constant companion, guiding us through the storms and trials of life. His love and grace are unending, offering us comfort and strength in times of need.

As we navigate the challenges of this world, we can find comfort in the knowledge that our Savior has already overcome the world. His sacrifice on the cross has paved the way for our salvation, and through Him, we can find peace and eternal life.

In the face of uncertainty, we can hold onto the hope that comes from knowing Jesus Christ. His promise of salvation is a beacon of light in the darkness, offering us a way forward and a reason to keep pressing on.

So, let us approach the Lord with open hearts and minds, seeking His guidance and grace. Let us call upon His name and trust in His unfailing love. In doing so, we can find the strength to face life's challenges and the assurance of a future filled with hope and joy.

July 25

Jeremiah 4:4

God longs for a connection with you. You are cherished by Him. Therefore, when you divert your attention to other matters above and before Him, it causes Him pain and provokes His anger. He is a jealous God (Exodus 20:5-6), not in the worldly sense of jealousy.

God's jealousy for you stems from His desire for what is best for you - which is Him and His divine plans for your life. Anything else leads to death and ruin. Anything apart from what the Lord has in store for you is deceitful and a tool used to distance you from God.

In essence, none of those worldly pursuits are worthwhile. You must honestly assess your life and cleanse your heart. This involves consciously and willingly eliminating anything that hinders your relationship with your loving Father. It must be done with a genuine and humble heart.

God may allow you to face the consequences of your poor decisions, but for those who consistently prioritize Him, He will not only bestow blessings but also blessings for future generations.

July 26

Lamentations 3:25

Before I surrendered my life to Jesus, I was lost in a cycle of self-destruction and chaos. I was constantly seeking fulfillment in all the wrong places, only to be left feeling empty and broken. But once I made the decision to fully commit my heart to Jesus, everything changed. I found a sense of peace and purpose that I had never experienced before.

I can now see how God was always there, trying to guide me back on the right path whenever I strayed. It's like He's a loving Father, patiently cleaning up after His messy children. And even though I still make mistakes, I strive to live a life that honors Him and brings Him glory. Whenever I do stumble, I know that I can always turn to my Heavenly Father for help and guidance.

God always listens to my prayers, comforts me in times of need, and helps me move forward with grace and strength. His goodness and faithfulness never waver, even when His timing may not align with my own. My hope and trust are firmly rooted in Him, knowing that He has a perfect plan for my life and will never leave me nor forsake me.

July 27

Ezekiel 34:16

There are numerous leaders across the globe who are failing to uphold what is righteous and just as per God's teachings. The famous saying, "the bigger they are, the harder they fall" will surely ring true when God decides to intervene.

Holding a position of leadership entails immense responsibility. It signifies that there are individuals observing and emulating them, and if they are guiding people astray, they are causing them to stumble and lose their way.

God has promised that He will eventually come and deal with leaders who are leading His followers down the wrong path and suppressing them, regardless of how powerful or influential they may seem. True justice will prevail, and God Himself will look after His followers to provide healing and strength.

This applies not only to world leaders, but to all leaders, whether they are Kings, Presidents, Priests, Judges, Law Enforcement, or News Anchors. God is watching, God is concerned, and God will hold everyone answerable for the path they lead His people on, and for the care and justice they either provided or withheld.

Genesis 1:27

We are a reflection of the love of God Himself. Since God is flawless in every aspect, it follows that we are created in the image of perfection. We possess the capacity to create, destroy, love, think, choose, and much more.

Just as God reigns over us, we are intended to rule over creation. Like God, we consist of a spirit, soul, and body. We are lovingly fashioned in the likeness of the most magnificent being of all.

Understanding this truth makes it difficult to perceive ourselves in any other light. The devil would prefer you to see yourself differently. Therefore, whenever you doubt your worth or feel inadequate, remember whose image you bear.

The potential within us is boundless. God did not create us as an afterthought; each of us was meticulously and purposefully crafted. God does not make mistakes.

So, when you are feeling low, recall the love that was infused into your creation and that you mirror the image of your Father, the Creator of Heaven and Earth.

July 29

Judges 6:12-16

Throughout history, God has consistently chosen the underdog to display His power and glory. From the story of David and Goliath to the humble beginnings of Jesus Christ, God has shown a preference for using those who are overlooked by the world to achieve remarkable triumphs.

It is through the ordinary individuals, like you and me, that God executes His divine plan, leaving others in awe of His power.

There have been times when I have doubted my abilities when God called me to action, but I have come to realize that it is not about my own capabilities.

Instead of questioning, I now place my trust in Him and His plan for me. Despite our imperfections, God utilizes us to bring about incredible victories daily.

If you ever feel unworthy or unprepared to fulfill your purpose, remember that God can work miracles through you. Have faith and trust in His plan, and witness the miraculous work of the Almighty in your life.

July 30

1 Chronicles 29:12

My husband and I enjoy contemplating what we would do if we were to win the lottery. As we have grown older, our aspirations have shifted towards things like going on an extended riverboat cruise, assisting our family in achieving stability, owning a coffee roastery, and traveling frequently.

Despite allowing our minds to wander and indulge in these daydreams, we do not linger there for too long. We always return to reality, look around, and express gratitude to God for His blessings and provisions. We are genuinely thankful for all that He provides. We recognize that God meets all our needs, and sometimes even provides extras.

My husband is a Captain Paramedic and has been serving in this field for 30 years. His work has been both a blessing and has blessed him. I am a Christian Author and advocate for those struggling with addiction, abuse, incarceration, and more, and my work has also been a blessing and has blessed me.

We both understand and value the fact that the lives we lead are by God's grace and provision, and that it is He who gives us the strength to carry on.

Psalms 1:3-4

This passage serves as a powerful reminder of the importance of faith and trust in God. By building our lives upon Him, we are able to weather any storm that comes our way.

Just as a house needs a strong foundation to withstand the elements, so too do we need a strong foundation in the Lord to navigate the challenges of life.

Those who put their trust in God will find peace and strength in the midst of chaos, knowing that He is always there to guide and protect them.

On the other hand, those who choose to live without a solid foundation in God will find themselves constantly searching for fulfillment in all the wrong places, only to come up empty-handed.

In the end, it is only through a deep and abiding relationship with God that we can truly experience His blessings and find lasting joy and contentment.

August

August 1

Proverbs 3:5-6

This scripture from the Bible has always been my grandmother's guiding light. Throughout my life, whenever I faced uncertainty or burdens, she would recite it to me.

I have always admired her resilience, having overcome numerous challenges such as early motherhood, abuse, abandonment, infidelity, loss of loved ones to cancer, raising children not her own, earning a degree, and never wavering in her faith in Jesus.

Despite not knowing how she would make it through each day, she held onto her faith and God always provided. Her emphasis on not relying solely on our own understanding has taught me to surrender to the Lord's will, trusting Him to guide our paths and not waste time and energy on pursuits not meant for us.

I am grateful for the lessons in faith, wisdom, and grace that my grandmother has imparted to me, and I thank God for blessing me with her presence in my life.

August 2

Daniel 10:19

Sometimes a few words of encouragement can help you regain your focus and motivation. You might be feeling tired, worn out, overwhelmed, or scared, but God is urging you to stop and take a breath.

There is nothing to be afraid of - not death, illness, or the unknown. His love and grace are all around you, waiting for you to embrace them. God is faithful and His words are true.

The Bible is His way of encouraging you to keep moving forward in life. It offers peace for your soul and strength for your tired body. You are His beloved, and every moment with you is precious to Him.

If you're struggling, open your Bible and listen to His voice. Let His message penetrate your doubts and fears, and walk in the light and truth of His presence in your life.

He will never leave you, but you are on a journey back to Him, and He is loving you, providing for you, and guiding you to His throne.

August 3

Jeremiah 9:24

My granddaughter came to spend the summer with me, and as she connected her phone to my car, a series of rap songs started playing loudly from my speakers. These songs boasted proudly about material possessions such as big houses, large bank accounts, multiple women on speed dial, copious amounts of drugs, and overpriced cars.

All I could think was, "how unoriginal." And then I thought, "Who would these rappers be without all these things?" So, as the music played, we decided to lower the volume for a moment and sing our own version of a rap song, making light of the situation and changing the music genre altogether.

I did my best to impart to her the values that truly matter in life, such as God, family, self-control, monogamy, and much more. Throughout her visit, I wanted her to witness God's presence in my life and how my husband and I recognize that every good thing in our lives, including her, is by God's grace. All gifts from above, given with love.

If I boast about any of these gifts, it's because I know who sent them and where they came from. Nothing good that I have is something I obtained apart from Him.

August 4

Matthew 10:29-31

Human beings are a unique creation of God, placed above all other creations to govern them as God governs us. God has meticulously crafted every living thing and cares deeply for everything He has created, from the smallest to the largest.

Consider how much more He cares for us, placing us above all other creations and paying special attention to even the tiniest creatures such as sparrows, ants, and bees. Nothing escapes His knowledge.

We are invaluable. Even the number of hairs on our heads is known to Him. Have you ever tried counting the hairs on your head, or the hairs of every human on Earth? It's quite remarkable! Our worth is derived from the sacrifice of Jesus Christ on the cross.

We are so precious to God that He sent a part of Himself in human form to live, teach, suffer, die, and be resurrected, providing us with a way to return to Him. We were headed in the opposite direction, but because of our Father's attention, affection, love, and dedication, we once again have hope.

August 5

John 13:34-35

Love is the foundation of our faith and the essence of our relationship with God. It is through love that we are able to connect with others and show them the light of Christ. Our love for one another is a powerful testimony to the world of the transformative power of God's love in our lives. It is a beacon of hope in a world filled with darkness and despair.

As we walk in love, we are called to be a reflection of Christ to those around us. Our actions and words should be a testament to the love that God has shown us, and a reminder of the sacrifice that Jesus made for us on the cross. By loving one another, we are fulfilling the greatest commandment that Jesus gave us - to love God with all our heart, soul, and mind, and to love our neighbors as ourselves.

Love is the antidote to hate and division, and it is through love that we are able to bring healing and reconciliation to a broken world.

Let us put aside our differences and come together in unity and love, for it is through our love for one another that the world will know that we are followers of Christ. Love is the greatest sign of our faith, and it is through love that we are able to bring glory to God in all that we do.

August 6

Romans 8:26

I recall the day my second son entered the world. My pregnancy had been quite challenging due to a diagnosis of pre-eclampsia, which led to strict bedrest for the final three months.

Balancing this with caring for my first son while my husband was at work was no easy feat. Then, unexpectedly, my husband left me late in my pregnancy, only to return shortly before giving birth. The stress, fluid retention, and frequent premature labor scares and hospital stays took a toll on me.

After eighteen and a half hours of labor, my son was born, but the joy was overshadowed by the medical team's urgent actions to save him. The cord was wrapped around his neck, and he was unresponsive. As they rushed him away, my husband and I sat in silence, fearing the worst.

Eventually, the doctor returned with the news that our son was alive, a moment where prayers were answered without words. Trust in faith, for sometimes prayers are heard in the silence of our hearts.

1 Corinthians 15:55

Before I found salvation, I faced numerous challenges that threatened to destroy me, but one stood out above all - my addiction. I fell into drug addiction at 33 and ended up in prison by 36. It was a tool of the enemy, and due to my lack of knowledge and faith, it almost overcame me.

However, as my mind cleared in prison and I accepted Jesus as my Savior, my thirst for God's word became unquenchable. I started memorizing scriptures and spending hours reading the Bible daily. Eventually, I stumbled upon a verse that asked, "Where, O death, is your victory?" It resonated with me and my circumstances.

I realized that through God's grace, I may have been knocked down, but I wasn't defeated. I may have been wounded, but I wasn't dead. God had already started the process of healing and binding my wounds.

He turned what the devil meant for harm into a testimony of His glory and a source of hope for others. God breathed life into the places where death tried to claim me, and He marked those places as His own. Wherever God is present, there is always hope and life.

Ephesians 5:15

If you were to give up your life for someone you deeply care about, how would you wish for them to spend the rest of their days? You wouldn't want them to waste the precious sacrifice you made for them. You would want them to embrace every opportunity to live a fulfilling and righteous life, while also helping others do the same.

The time we have on this Earth is a valuable gift bestowed upon us by love. Jesus desires the same for us through His sacrifice. He wants us to make wise choices, follow what is good, and be responsible stewards of the time we have been given, living according to His purpose for us.

There are plenty of sources to guide us in making the right decisions, such as Jesus, the Bible, life experiences, and the outcomes of people's choices. You have everything you need to lead a life full of love, hope, and blessings.

The Holy Spirit, our ultimate guide, resides within us. Let us not be controlled by the temptations of the world, but instead cherish the life that was sacrificed for us above all else and make the most of the time we have left.

August 9

Psalms 130:3-4

The passage exudes a profound sense of longing. The psalmist earnestly prays from the depths of their heart and pain, expressing confidence and hope that God will hear and respond.

They also recognize that God's love, grace, and forgiveness are the only things that can completely erase our transgressions as if they never existed. This does not mean that there are no consequences for our sins, but rather that the debt has been paid through Jesus Christ's blood, and God no longer holds it against us.

We cannot even begin to count the number of sins in our lifetime, and once we are saved, not even God keeps track of them. They are paid for all eternity, including our past, present, and future sins.

Sin inevitably leads to suffering. The psalmist is keenly aware of this truth in their own life, and approaches God humbly and repentantly.

Sin sends out waves of suffering, causing devastation to all those in its path, but God is able to intervene if we approach Him with godly fear and reverence, seeking Him above all else.

Isaiah 6:8

Remember the feeling of sitting in class and waiting for someone to raise their hand with an answer when the teacher asked a question?

Most of the time, everyone looked around to see who would be the brave one to lift up their hand, or they looked down at their desk hoping the teacher wouldn't call on them because no one volunteered.

Occasionally, someone would rise to the occasion and the classroom felt a sigh of relief. We should all aspire to be like the brave child who responded to the teacher. The child who had prepared themselves by studying and doing their homework.

As children of God, we should always be prepared to give an answer when duty calls, and we should be the first ones volunteering to be sent out into God's field to harvest His crop.

All you have to do is show up, and follow God's lead. Let the Holy Spirit guide you and you will walk into blessings that you could never have imagined.

August 11

Hosea 6:1

The seven years I spent behind bars were some of the most challenging and transformative years of my life. I was separated from my loved ones, forced to adapt to the harsh conditions of prison life, and faced with the reality of my past mistakes every day. However, through this adversity, I found a new perspective on life.

I learned to cherish the simple joys of freedom, the warmth of family, and the abundance of blessings that I had previously taken for granted. My faith in God was tested, but ultimately strengthened, as I found solace in His love and guidance during my darkest moments.

The discipline and refinement I experienced were painful, but necessary for my personal growth and redemption. I believe that God used this time to shape me into a better person, and to guide me towards a greater purpose. I am committed to living a life of gratitude, humility, and service, and I am determined to make the most of the second chance that I have been given.

So, don't get upset or be discouraged when the Lord corrects you. See it as a demonstration of His love, commitment, and involvement in your life, guiding you towards something better.

August 12

Luke 15:7

Salvation holds great significance. All of Heaven celebrates when even a single individual decides to embrace the salvation offered by our Lord Jesus Christ. It is a beautiful and intimate moment, as well as a profound victory for the Kingdom of God.

We were once like lost sheep, and our Holy Shepherd sought us out to bring us back home. Heaven eagerly awaits the news of the Lord's return with His flock. However, the focus of this scripture is on repentance.

Jesus came for us, but we must actively choose to return to Him and not continue to stray. The Creator is wooing us to come back home, and once we accept this invitation, it is truly something to rejoice in. Can you imagine the celebration in Heaven? I hope to experience it one day.

Jesus never disregarded anyone, despite being the King of all Kings. He came as a humble servant, interacting and dining with the lowly, demonstrating that everyone is deserving of love. God cares for each and every one of us. Let His boundless love be the focus of your thoughts today.

August 13

John 14:2

Life is a journey filled with twists and turns, highs and lows, and unexpected challenges. It's easy to get caught up in the worries and stresses of everyday life, from financial struggles to health issues to relationship problems. But amidst all the chaos and uncertainty, there is a glimmer of hope that shines brightly - the promise of eternal life in Heaven.

No matter what struggles we face on Earth, we can find solace in the fact that this world is not our final destination. Jesus has gone before us to prepare a place for us in His Father's house, a place where there is no pain, no sorrow, no death, and no tears. It is a place of eternal peace and joy, where we will be reunited with loved ones and bask in the presence of our Savior.

So, when life gets tough and the road ahead seems daunting, remember the promise of Heaven that awaits us. Let it be a source of comfort and strength, knowing that our struggles here on Earth are only temporary, and that a glorious eternity in the presence of God awaits us. Keep your eyes fixed on the prize, and trust in the hope that is found in Jesus Christ.

August 14

Romans 12:16

We are called to be the hands and feet of Jesus, spreading His message of love and compassion to those around us. Just as Jesus did not seek to be served, but to serve, we too should humble ourselves and look for opportunities to help those less fortunate.

Whether it's volunteering at a local shelter, visiting the sick and elderly, or simply lending a listening ear to someone in need, we can make a difference in the lives of others.

By following Jesus' example of selflessness and love, we can bring hope and healing to a broken world. Let us not be content with simply attending church on Sundays, but let us actively seek ways to make a positive impact in our communities.

As we reach out to others with genuine care and dedication, we can openly reflect the heart of Jesus and bring light into the darkness. Let us be bold in our faith and show the world the transformative power of God's love.

August 15

2 Corinthians 10:5

Our minds are constantly bombarded with thoughts that do not align with God's will. These thoughts can be negative, like envy, jealousy, hate, or lust. However, we must not let them control us. Instead, we can use the spiritual gifts given to us by God to fight against these thoughts. It's like facing a tough pitch from the devil, but we have the word of God as our bat to hit it out of the park and claim victory in Christ!

When we allow negative thoughts to take root in our minds, it can lead us down a path of destruction and separation from God. We must be vigilant in guarding our minds and hearts against these harmful thoughts, and instead, fill them with the truth of God's word and the promises He has given us. By relying on the power of prayer, scripture, and the Holy Spirit, we can combat these negative thoughts and align ourselves with God's will for our lives.

It's important to remember that we are not alone in this battle against sinful thoughts. God has equipped us with spiritual gifts to overcome them and live a life that is pleasing to Him. By leaning on Him and trusting in His strength, we can overcome any negative thought that comes our way and walk in victory as children of God.

August 16

Matthew 11:29

When we choose to take on Jesus' yoke, we are choosing to walk in His footsteps and follow His teachings. This means living a life of love, compassion, forgiveness, and service to others. It means surrendering our own will and desires to His, trusting that His way is the path to true fulfillment and joy.

Taking on Jesus' yoke also means finding rest for our souls. In a world filled with chaos, stress, and uncertainty, His yoke offers us a sense of peace and security that can only come from a deep relationship with Him. It is a reminder that we do not have to carry our burdens alone, but can lean on Him for strength and guidance.

Ultimately, embracing Jesus' yoke is a choice to live a life of purpose and meaning. It is a commitment to walk in His light and share His love with the world. And as we do so, we can experience the abundant life that He promises to all who follow Him.

August 17

Proverbs 25:21

We are all familiar with the phrase "kill them with kindness." This passage echoes a similar sentiment. It’s easy to help a stranger or a friend in need, but when it comes to an enemy, it becomes more challenging. Nevertheless, we should still do it. If you come across an enemy struggling and have the means to help, take the opportunity to glorify God, spread love, drive out hate, and perhaps even make a new friend in the process.

It's a win all the way around. I once had a woman who was very dear to me. However, she ended up betraying me in a significant way. The betrayal created a deep divide, and I wasn't sure if I could ever forgive her, nor did she ask for forgiveness. Years later, she faced a series of hardships, including divorce, family problems, financial issues, and the loss of a child.

Despite everything she had done to me, my heart ached for the burdens she was carrying, so I made the decision to reach out and offer her my help and friendship in any way I could. It was not easy, and onlookers couldn't comprehend how I could forgive her, but I did it anyway. I recalled all the times the Lord had forgiven me for the unforgivable, and I chose love above all else.

August 18

Psalms 143:10

I've made plenty of mistakes in my life, and the most difficult thing was forgiving myself. It was a journey in itself, and something life-changing and miraculous came out of that experience. When I finally turned to the Lord and accepted His forgiveness, I started the climb up the mountain of self-forgiveness.

I followed Jesus all the way to the top, and when I reached it, everything changed. I learned to love myself again, set healthy boundaries, and not let the world's labels define who God says I am. I learned from my mistakes, chose to keep following Jesus, and moved forward with my life. I had strayed from God's path and stumbled, but the Lord picked me up and turned me around. All I had to do was keep moving forward.

He has brought me to a steady place in life, and through His word, He has taught me how to live according to His will. I still have moments when I trip over my own feet, so to speak, but I continue to reach out to Jesus, take His hand, get back up, and keep going. His Spirit knows the way home, and it lives inside of us, so we are never really lost. We just have to stop seeing with our eyes and start seeing through His grace.

August 19

Zephaniah 3:20

God is an expert at restoring things. He has taken those who were rejected and used humble people throughout history, lifting them up to a position that the world could not deny was the work of God. He enjoys doing this. He has intervened and brought His people together when the world and its leaders tried their best to suppress and divide them.

God is also capable of working in your life in similar ways. You might feel like you have nothing left to give, or you might be at rock bottom with no hope of climbing back up, but there is always a way - The Way, in fact. And The Way has a name - Immanuel, or God with us.

The truth is, we can't do it on our own, but the other truth is that we don't have to. He lives within us, filled with the same power that raised Him from the dead, glorified Him, and brought Him back to His rightful place in Heaven. All you have to do is believe, follow, and receive. We may doubt ourselves, but we should never doubt our all-powerful Father who loves us beyond imagination.

August 20

John 5:14

Sometimes we find ourselves so lost in our sinfulness that we can't see a way out. We may ask for help from those around us, but that doesn't always work. However, when Jesus enters the picture, everything changes.

Just before Jesus healed a man who had been paralyzed for decades, He asked the man if he genuinely wanted to be healed. The man didn't respond with a resounding "yes," but instead complained about how no one else would help him. Jesus told the man to get up and help himself - to carry his own mat and walk. Jesus provided the healing, but the man had to get up and walk.

Later, Jesus found the man in the temple and warned him that if he continued to sin, something worse might happen. God will always meet us where we are and provide the resources we need to do His will, but we have to get up and take action.

We can't just sit around and wait for someone else to fix our problems, nor can we keep making the same mistakes. We must use the gifts we've been given, have faith, and be thankful to bring about the healing we long for in our lives.

August 21

Philippians 4:6-7

There are numerous things that could occupy our minds and waste our time and energy today. Whether it's financial issues, political concerns, or even just deciding what to wear, there's no need to stress. Instead of worrying, we can turn our concerns into prayers that will be answered.

Worrying is like knocking on a locked door with no one behind it, but when we pray to God, the door is always open. With practice, choosing which door to knock on becomes easier and eventually becomes second nature. You can knock on God's door once, receive the peace He offers, and go about your day worry-free, or you can waste your time banging on a door that will never open - the choice is yours.

The passage above is an invitation from love Himself to surrender your troubles to Him. This act requires incredible faith and allows our burdens to be lifted from our hearts and minds and placed into His capable hands. By trusting in Him more than our fears, we are freed from the things that once held us back. So, when anxiety creeps in, take a deep breath and recall how the Lord has guided you through dark times in the past.

August 22

Nahum 1:7

The book of Nahum is a powerful reminder of God's faithfulness and protection over His people. In times of trouble and distress, we can find solace in knowing that God is our ultimate comforter and refuge. Just as Nahum's name means comforter, God offers us comfort and peace in the midst of our struggles. He is always there to guide us and lead us to safety.

When we witness the suffering of others, it is our duty to be a source of light and hope for them, pointing them towards God's love and protection. God is always watching over us, ready to defend His name and bring honor to it in unexpected ways. He is a loving and caring creator who cherishes each and every one of us, taking our concerns to heart.

Having a personal relationship with God means trusting in His unfailing love and turning to Him in times of need. Even when we face failure or betrayal from others, God remains steadfast and faithful. He is the one who will never let us down, offering us rest and peace for our weary souls. Let us find comfort and strength in God's presence, knowing that He is always there for us.

Isaiah 8:18

Let us strive to live in such a way that others see Jesus in us, not just through our words but through our actions and the way we treat others. Let us be known for our love, compassion, and forgiveness, just as Jesus was during His time on earth. Let us be willing to step out in faith and share the good news of salvation with those who are lost and hurting. Let us be willing to sacrifice our own comfort and desires in order to serve others and bring glory to God.

As followers of Jesus, we are called to be salt and light in the world that is in desperate need of both. Let us not be afraid to stand up for what is right and speak out against injustice and oppression. Let us be bold in our faith and unashamed of the gospel, knowing that it has the power to transform lives and bring hope to the hopeless.

In all that we do, let us seek to bring honor and glory to God, knowing that our lives are a reflection of His love and grace. Let us be faithful in our witness, knowing that God is always with us, guiding and empowering us to be His hands and feet in a broken and hurting world. Let us be living testimonies of the power of God to change lives and bring about redemption and restoration.

August 24

Exodus 20:16

By choosing to live a life of honesty and transparency, we not only honor God but also build a foundation of trust and respect in our relationships. When we speak the truth in love, we create a safe and nurturing environment where open communication can flourish. This allows for genuine connections to be formed, based on mutual respect and understanding.

Furthermore, by being truthful and accountable in our actions, we set a positive example for others to follow. Our integrity and honesty can inspire those around us to do the same, creating a ripple effect of authenticity and trustworthiness in our communities.

In a world where deceit and dishonesty seem to be prevalent, it is more important than ever for believers to stand firm in their commitment to truth and integrity. By upholding these values, we not only honor God but also contribute to a more compassionate and understanding society. Let us strive to be beacons of truth and light in a world that is often clouded by deception and falsehood.

Esther 9:22

I can still recall the exact moment when I made the life-changing decision to surrender myself to Jesus. The instant I entrusted my life to Him is forever etched into my being. It felt as though a heavy burden had been lifted off my shoulders, replaced by a profound sense of joy, hope, relief, and happiness.

I shared my newfound freedom with the women around me, praising God for His boundless grace and mercy. It was indeed a moment worth rejoicing! In that moment, my adversary, who is also God's adversary, suffered a significant defeat.

The Lord transformed my sadness into gladness, and my mourning into a day of celebration. As followers of Christ, we can wake up each day celebrating the precious gift of life, cherishing moments spent with loved ones, and showing care for the needs of others.

Although salvation is freely given, it came at a great cost. After embracing Jesus as our Lord and Savior, every day can be viewed as the greatest day of our lives, because it truly is!

August 26

Deuteronomy 4:39

God's presence is not limited to a distant, far-off place like Heaven. He is here, right now, in the midst of our daily struggles and triumphs. He is not a passive observer, but an active participant in our lives, walking alongside us through every trial and tribulation.

When we choose to follow God, we are not alone in our journey. He goes before us, clearing the path and making a way where there seems to be no way. His blessings overflow in our lives, even in the face of adversity and opposition. As long as we keep our eyes fixed on Him, nothing can hinder His plans for us.

God's will is perfect and sovereign, orchestrating every detail of our lives for our ultimate good and His glory. He is the one true God, the Alpha and Omega, the Beginning and the End.

His love is a beacon of hope and salvation, drawing us closer to Him and leading others to the same saving grace. In God, we find true fulfillment and purpose, for He alone is the source of all life and goodness.

August 27

Psalms 4:4

It's important to recognize that anger is a complex emotion that can stem from a variety of sources, such as past trauma, unmet expectations, or feelings of injustice. It's crucial to address the root causes of our anger and work towards healing and resolution. This may involve seeking Christian therapy, practicing self-awareness, and developing healthy coping mechanisms.

In addition, it's important to communicate our feelings of anger in a respectful and constructive manner. This involves expressing our emotions assertively, rather than aggressively, and actively listening to the perspectives of others. By doing so, we can work towards finding common ground and resolving conflicts in a peaceful and productive way.

Ultimately, managing anger requires a conscious effort to cultivate patience, empathy, and understanding. It's a journey of self-discovery and personal growth, and it's important to remember that we are all capable of change and transformation. With faith and perseverance, we can learn to navigate our anger in a way that aligns with God’s will, ultimately leading to greater peace and harmony in our lives.

Isaiah 50:4

When we start our day with God's word, we are setting the tone for the rest of our day. We are arming ourselves with the truth and promises of God, which serve as a shield against the negativity and challenges that may come our way.

The insights and revelations we receive from our time with God can be shared with those around us, offering them hope and guidance in their own struggles. Just as CPR breathes life into someone in need, sharing God's word can breathe life and hope into the lives of others.

Prioritizing daily communion with God also demonstrates our faithfulness and commitment to Him. It shows that we recognize the importance of seeking His presence and guidance in our lives, and that we are willing to put Him first above all else.

Ultimately, spending time in God’s word equips us to be vessels of His love, grace, and truth, and empowers us to make a positive impact in the world, positioning ourselves to be lights in the darkness and agents of change in the lives of those we encounter.

August 29

Proverbs 31:30

God's standard of beauty for women is not based on outward appearances, but on her reverence for the Lord. I take advantage of the time my granddaughter spends with me during the summer to not only have fun with girly activities, but also to instill in her the qualities of a godly woman.

I want her to understand that true beauty comes from within, from a heart that is pure and a spirit that is aligned with God's will. I want her to know that her worth is not determined by society's standards or by how she looks, but by her character and her relationship with the Lord.

I want her to be confident in who she is, knowing that she is fearfully and wonderfully made by God, and I want her to embrace her uniqueness and not compare herself to others, understanding that she is loved and cherished just as she is.

I want her to be a woman of integrity, standing firm in her faith and living out God's truth in all areas of her life. I pray that as she grows and matures, she will continue to seek after God's heart and strive to be the woman He has called her to be. And I trust that with His guidance and grace, she will become a beautiful reflection of His love and grace to those around her.

August 30

Ecclesiastes 11:10

This message is a reminder for both the young and the old about how to live and die well. It urges us to focus on things that truly matter in life, rather than chasing after temporary pleasures. Let's pursue everlasting joy and seek our Creator, understanding the value of things beyond just their prices.

Let's not get caught up in the hustle and bustle of everyday life, but instead, take a step back and appreciate the beauty of the present moment. Let's prioritize experiences over possessions, kindness over competition, and love over hate. Let's make a conscious effort to be present, to listen deeply, and to connect authentically with those around us.

Let's not wait for tomorrow to start living our best lives, but instead, let's seize the day and make the most of every opportunity that comes our way. Let's be grateful for all that we have, and let's strive to make a positive impact on the world around us.

Let's remember that our time on this earth is precious and limited, and let's make the most of it by living with intention and purpose, leaving a legacy of love, kindness, and compassion that will continue to inspire others long after we are gone.

August 31

Matthew 5:14

When we allow Jesus to dwell in our hearts, His transformative power begins to work within us. His light shines through us, illuminating the darkness and bringing hope to those around us. As we walk in His light, we become agents of change in a world that is desperately in need of His love and grace.

We are called to be salt and light in a world that is often filled with bitterness and darkness. Just as salt preserves and enhances flavor, we are called to bring out the best in others and to preserve the truth of God's word. Our lives should be a reflection of His love, mercy, and grace, drawing others to Him through our actions and words.

As children of God, we are called to be ambassadors of His kingdom, spreading the good news of the gospel wherever we go. We are called to be a light in the darkness, a beacon of hope in a world that is often filled with despair. Our lives should be a testimony to the power of God's love and the transformation that He can bring.

Let us not be afraid to shine brightly for Jesus, even in the face of adversity. Let us be bold in our faith, knowing that He is with us every step of the way.

September

September 1

John 14:21

It is through our actions that we can show our love for God and for others. Just as Jesus demonstrated His love for us through His sacrifice on the cross, we are called to show our love for Him through our obedience and service to others. Love is not just a feeling, but a choice that we make every day to put others before ourselves and to follow God's word.

When we love God with all our heart, soul, and mind, we can experience the fullness of His love and presence in return. Our relationship with God is strengthened as we seek to live according to His will and to love others as He loves us. Through prayer, worship, and acts of kindness, we can show our gratitude for the love that God has shown us.

As we continue to grow in our love for God, we are transformed by His grace and mercy. Our hearts are filled with joy and peace, knowing that we are loved unconditionally by our Heavenly Father. Love is a powerful force that has the ability to heal, restore, and transform lives. By embracing the love of God and sharing it with others, we can experience the true meaning of love in all its beauty and wonder.

2 Corinthians 7:1

After you finish showering and cleansing yourself from all the dirt and grime, the last thing you'd want to do is go outside and roll around in the mud. The Lord has purified you from all your sins, now all He requests is that you don't return to the same mud puddles that made you dirty in the first place, and to steer clear of any new ones.

Just as the Lord sacrificed His life for you, we should dedicate our lives to Him as a way of expressing gratitude for His love, devotion, commitment, and grace.

I urge you today to evaluate the aspects of your life, your heart, and your mind, including your goals and aspirations, and ask yourself if they align with God's will. Are they driven by selfish desires, or do they honor God?

Seek God's guidance on your priorities, and ask Him to remove what doesn't belong, and to lead you towards what does, bringing glory to you so that you may glorify Him in return. Pray that the Lord guides you away from temptation and helps you avoid deliberate sins.

September 3

Proverbs 4:25

In life, just like in baseball, we face challenges, obstacles, and setbacks. But it's how we respond to these challenges that ultimately determines our success. We need to have resilience, determination, and a positive mindset to overcome any curveballs that come our way. Just like a baseball player needs to adjust their swing to hit a curveball, we need to adapt and learn in order to grow and improve.

Just as a baseball team works together to achieve a common goal, we need to surround ourselves with a supportive community and rely on others for help and guidance. We can't do it all on our own, and having a strong support system can make all the difference in reaching our goals and fulfilling our potential.

And just like in baseball, there will be times when we strike out or make errors. But it's important to remember that failure is not the end of the game - it's just a part of the process. We need to learn from our mistakes, make adjustments, and keep moving forward. As long as we stay focused, determined, and committed to our goals, we can overcome any obstacles and achieve success in the game of life.

September 4

Psalms 37:8

Looking back on my life, I can see how my impulsive decisions and lack of patience led me down paths I wish I hadn't taken. There were moments when I let fear and worry cloud my judgment, causing me to make choices that I now regret.

It wasn't until I turned to my faith and sought guidance from my Savior that I realized the power of surrendering control and trusting in a higher power. I learned that worrying about the future only steals the joy and peace that can be found in the present moment.

By following the teachings of Jesus and having faith in His plan for me, I was able to let go of my anxieties and embrace a more peaceful and fulfilling life. I now understand that challenges will always arise, but it is how we respond to them that defines who we are.

The choice is ours to either succumb to stress or to have faith and trust in our unwavering Lord, who promises to never let us down and assures us that everything will ultimately work out for our good as long as we prioritize seeking Him above all else.

September 5

Job 28:28

It's important to recognize that wisdom is not just about knowledge or intelligence, but also about humility and a willingness to learn. No matter how much we think we know, there is always more to learn.

True wisdom comes from acknowledging our limitations and being open to new ideas. The world's definition of wisdom is a far cry from God's definition.

According to the Bible, true wisdom comes from a deep reverence and awe for God. It involves trusting in Him, following His will, and living a life that reflects His love and grace.

This kind of wisdom is not about being the smartest or most successful person, but about living in a way that honors and glorifies God.

Living in fear of the Lord means acknowledging His sovereignty and trusting in His plans, even when we may not understand them. This kind of wisdom leads to a life filled with hope, peace, and a deeper understanding of God's love and purpose for our lives.

September 6

Genesis 50:20

Everyone has a unique story, and as I reflect on mine, I can now see that what God has planned for me is far greater than I could have ever imagined.

There were many moments when I thought I wouldn't make it, but somehow, I did. I survived serious health issues, domestic violence, time in prison, sexual abuse, drug addiction, and more. I never would have thought that God would use my experiences and voice to help save lives.

He has worked through me in ministry, mentoring, writing, public speaking, volunteering, fundraising, and in many other ways. God can do the impossible through those who seem like a lost cause.

I have faced many fears and even some ridicule, but when I feel God's call, I respond and watch Him work miracles. It has been a terrifying yet beautifully blessed experience.

I wake up each day excited to see what the Lord will bring into my life and where He will lead me. Exciting things happen when we invite the God of all mercy and grace to show up and show out!

Psalms 20:4

When we align our hearts with God's, we open ourselves up to His abundant blessings and favor. By surrendering our plans and desires to Him, we allow Him to work in and through us, bringing about outcomes that exceed our wildest dreams.

It is important to continuously evaluate our motives and desires, ensuring that they are in line with God's will. When we seek to honor and glorify Him in all that we do, we position ourselves to receive His blessings and favor. This requires a deep level of trust and surrender, as we relinquish control and allow God to lead us towards His best for our lives.

Prayer becomes a powerful tool in aligning our hearts with the Lord's. By bringing our desires before Him and seeking His guidance, we invite Him to work in and through us, shaping our desires to agree with His perfect will. Additionally, praying for the desires of others demonstrates a selfless and loving heart, reflecting the character of Christ.

Ultimately, a heart that seeks after God above all else will experience the fullness of His presence and blessings. By aligning our desires with His, we position ourselves to walk in His favor and experience the abundant life He has promised to those who love and serve Him.

Micah 7:18-19

You might feel like you've committed a sin that is too great to be forgiven, but that's not true. If that thought crosses your mind, it means you're underestimating the power, grace, and sacrifice of Jesus on the cross.

There is no sin in this world that cannot be forgiven if we come to the Lord with a humble heart, seeking His forgiveness. We just need to be willing to turn away from our wrongdoings and not look back.

Our God is a God of love, and love always wins! Even if He was upset with us momentarily, like a parent with their child, He is quick to forgive and show compassion.

If God can forgive us, we must also learn to forgive ourselves. To overcome the burden of unforgiveness, we must embrace the truth of salvation, and just like our heavenly Father, we should also forgive others as we have been forgiven.

September 9

Amos 5:24

God desires for us to live lives that align with our worship. Therefore, we should first ask ourselves, "Are we worshipping in a way that is pleasing to God?"

Secondly, we need to ask, "Are we living in accordance with the way we worship?" Honoring the Lord goes beyond attending church on Sundays. We must be righteous in both our worship and our daily lives.

Our treatment of others, our compassion for those in need, and the sincerity of our hearts all reflect our true relationship and intentions with God. Our love should not only be expressed in words, but also in our actions, and it should be genuine.

God wants our righteousness to flow continuously in our daily lives and in our worship, never running dry, but overflowing into the dry ground around us, bringing forth a wellspring of life to places that seemed hopeless.

God is calling you; how will you respond?

September 10

Proverbs 21:3

As a parent and grandparent, I hope that the generations after me will learn from my mistakes and listen to the good advice I give them based on the lessons I've learned in life. This will help them avoid falling into the same traps that I did, or that others have fallen into.

It's important to prevent problems before they happen. It's much easier to keep your new white shirt clean than to try and remove stains later on. God wants us to have good morals as we go through life, which is why it's imperative to start teaching these values to our children and grandchildren early on.

Our inner motives must be genuine, as God places great value on sincerity. God gave us His word out of love and hope that we would take it to heart and put it into practice, so that we can live fulfilling lives that both satisfy and honor Him.

Just as a parent sets rules for their household, God has given us commandments to follow. These rules are in place as a sign of care and affection, in the hope that they are followed with love and respect for the one who wrote them.

September 11

Exodus 20:17

It's easy to get caught up in the hustle and bustle of everyday life, constantly striving for more and better things. We set goals and work tirelessly to achieve them, always looking towards the future and what we hope to attain. While ambition and drive are important qualities to have, it's equally important to take a step back and appreciate the blessings that we already have in our lives.

In our pursuit of success and material wealth, we often overlook the simple joys and blessings that surround us every day. Whether it's the love of family and friends, good health, a roof over our heads, or the beauty of nature, there are countless blessings that we should be grateful for. Taking the time to acknowledge and appreciate these blessings can bring a sense of contentment and fulfillment that material possessions can never provide.

Gratitude is a powerful tool that can shift our perspective and bring us closer to true happiness. By focusing on what we have rather than what we lack, we can cultivate a sense of abundance and joy in our lives. So, as we continue to strive for our goals and dreams, let's not forget to pause and give thanks for the blessings that already enrich our lives.

Isaiah 41:9

The words in this passage resonate deeply within my soul. The love that is described here is so pure and unconditional, it brings tears to my eyes. It is a love that transcends all boundaries and barriers, a love that is unwavering and eternal.

It is a love that is personal and intimate, a love that is meant for me and for you. To think that out of all the billions of people in the world, God has chosen each and every one of us individually.

He knows us by name, He knows our struggles and our triumphs, He knows the deepest desires of our hearts. And yet, despite all of our flaws and imperfections, He still chooses us.

It is a love that is so great, so overwhelming, that it led Him to send His only Son to die for us, to pave the way for us to be reunited with Him for eternity.

It is a love that never gives up on us, no matter how far we may have strayed. It is a love that is always there, waiting for us with open arms, ready to welcome us back into His embrace.

September 13

Matthew 26:41

I'm not sure about you, but it's been quite some time since I was in high school and college. I recall tackling all sorts of challenging math problems back then, but I couldn't explain how to solve the slope of an S line now. It's simply because I haven't been practicing or studying these concepts.

As the old saying goes, "if you don't use it, you lose it." The same principle applies to the word of God. Life is hectic and filled with distractions and temptations, so if we're not actively strengthening our spiritual and mental well-being to prepare for whatever challenges come our way, we're more likely to falter.

Despite our good intentions, our human nature is frail. We need to be alert and conscious, immersing ourselves in God's teachings for strength and direction, and remaining steadfast in prayer to maintain our connection with our Savior and God through the Holy Spirit's power to fend off the devil's schemes.

Even though a spiritual war is waged against us, we have been provided with every good resource from above to lead victorious lives that bring glory to our Father in Heaven.

September 14

Psalms 5:8

Who do you turn to for guidance and protection when facing opposition and hardship? When it feels like everything is working against you and your world is falling apart, do you rely on God in faith, or do you find yourself consumed with worry and fear? Or do you lose hope altogether?

David, a man who was close to God's heart, experienced struggles such as lust, parental issues, pride, and the everyday challenges of living in a broken world. Despite having enemies, he always knew to bring his troubles to God.

He trusted in God's word and believed that only the Lord could help him navigate life's worries. Instead of acting impulsively out of fear and worry, he approached God with reverence and patience, seeking His guidance and provision.

The path ahead may seem uncertain, but your loving Savior knows the way and will lead you through the darkness if you choose to hold His hand and follow Him in faith.

Job 19:25-27

We are privileged and fortunate to serve a Savior who has risen. He has triumphed over death and has promised us an everlasting life, free from suffering, death, and the chaos of this world.

We will experience the joy of glory for all eternity. When we reach our limits and exhaust ourselves, it is a perfect opportunity to step aside and allow the Lord to take control.

When the comfort of others brings no comfort at all, we can find true comfort in the one who offers us a peace that surpasses worldly offerings.

Our redeemer is alive! He is a steadfast foundation that we can always rely on when everything and everyone else disappoints us, even when we disappoint ourselves.

Therefore, when you find yourself at the end of your rope, remember that with the Lord, it is only just the beginning. With Him comes eternal life - the old will fade away, and the new will emerge.

September 16

2 Kings 6:16

The devil and his demons work tirelessly to deceive and manipulate us into believing that we are alone in our struggles, and that we are unworthy of love and grace. But the truth is, we are surrounded by a powerful army of angels who are constantly fighting on our behalf, and we have a loving God who is always by our side, ready to offer us comfort, strength, and guidance.

It's important to remember that we are never alone in our battles. We also have a community of believers who are there to support us, to lift us up in prayer, and to walk alongside us in our journey. When we feel overwhelmed by the darkness, we can call upon the name of Jesus and feel His presence surrounding us, filling us with peace and hope.

The devil may try to convince us that we are weak and powerless, but the truth is that we are children of the Most High God, created in His image and filled with His Spirit. We have the power to overcome any obstacle, to stand firm in our faith, and to walk in victory. So let us hold fast to the truth, let us cling to the promises of God, and let us walk boldly in the light of His love.

Proverbs 13:20

This scripture provides a straightforward explanation of the importance of choosing our friends wisely. The people we interact with daily have a significant impact on the course and quality of our lives.

Associating with wise individuals ensures a supportive network when we stray from the right path, and we, in turn, can offer wisdom to our friends if they lose their way.

Conversely, surrounding ourselves with those who engage in negative behaviors such as gossip, excessive drinking, violence, or promiscuity, and who lead worldly lives, does not bode well for us.

Just as we wouldn't seek financial advice from someone who has a history of poor financial decisions, we should seek guidance from those who have made wise investments and are successful.

This underscores the importance of surrounding ourselves with fellow believers, as they can help us stay aligned with God's will. We ourselves, must also embody God's grace and lead others towards His loving embrace.

September 18

Jeremiah 29:13-14

Every time I read these verses, it brings to mind everything I've been through in the past and how far God has brought me. I used to live a life full of sin that led me into captivity.

It was only when I started seeking the Lord and giving my heart completely over to Him that I began to experience a new kind of freedom. He broke the chains of sin that had been holding me captive for so long.

My physical captivity was a reflection of what was happening internally, and once God and I sorted out the internal struggles, I was given my physical freedom and returned home.

God and I found each other in an intimate embrace in the middle of the darkness, and once that happened, I never looked back. He took away any desire I would ever have to even want to.

God's promises are real, and I am living proof. What He has done in my life, He can do in yours. He can set you free and break the chains that hold you captive, but you must turn towards Him and seek Him above all else from your heart and never look back.

September 19

Deuteronomy 10:12-13

God is our husband, and marriage necessitates and craves wholehearted love, loyalty, and dedication. The Lord has bestowed upon us His all, and His very best, and it is understandable that He would seek the same in return from His bride. Despite our unfaithfulness, He has never given up on His marriage. He has only intensified His devotion to demonstrate that He is committed for the long term and will never leave, but He will not force us to choose Him because love cannot be forced.

The Lord never demands anything from us that He Himself hasn't already done to prove His commitment to His marriage. So, if you are experiencing or have experienced marital difficulties, take heart, even the Lord has marital challenges, but He, as a faithful spouse, is doing everything in His power to resolve them. He knows what's best for us, He simply wants us to recognize it and embrace this truth and all that it entails.

If you see someone you love walking blindly into a burning building, you will do everything in your power to get them to open their eyes and turn around. That is all our loving Husband is trying to get us to do, to awaken us from our selfish, obstinate ways, and embrace the grace and devotion of a faithful love.

September 20

Psalms 30:2

Even if a sheep strays from the flock, it remains under the care of the shepherd. No matter what, we are still under the protection of the Lord, and He watches over us.

Sickness, disease, or afflictions can have various causes. According to the Bible, they can result from our own sins, the sins of others, disobedience, or as a consequence of actions.

Sickness and death were not part of God's original plan for us, but they entered the world when sin entered the Garden of Eden. Since then, we have been waging war against them every day.

However, there is always hope, and I have personally witnessed its power. When all else fails, prayer is the ultimate solution. God is always ready to listen to our prayers for healing, and I have seen Him respond in miraculous ways.

He may wound, but He also binds up. God is our ultimate healer, the one we should seek in times of trouble. His words bring life and health to those who embrace them.

September 21

Ezekiel 36:26

One of the things I prioritize advocating for is the belief that people have the capacity to change. God is capable of accomplishing anything, including giving us new hearts that seek Him above all else.

I found myself seated at a dinner table with a group of law enforcement officers several months following my release from prison.

They commenced sharing anecdotes of triumph and making disparaging remarks about individuals they had apprehended, as well as making harsh comments about those grappling with addiction.

I eventually reached my limit and reminded them that I was one of the people they were speaking about. One of the people they had deemed as having no hope, yet there I was, transformed, seated at their dinner table, so transformed that they had forgotten I was ever a criminal in the first place.

They had to acknowledge the presence of God, and the reality that hope is never lost, and that we are all tasked with being stewards of this truth and God's grace.

September 22

Joel 2:12-13

This provides a glimmer of hope in situations where we realize we've made some mistakes. God assures us of His grace and mercy through His unwavering love if we come back to Him, forsaking our sins, and opening our hearts to Him.

He promises not to unleash the punishment we deserve, but instead, we will encounter His grace. God is patient, displaying His compassion towards us, desiring that we draw closer to Him daily and have faith in our Creator.

He demonstrates love towards us even when we are unworthy. God desires not only our outward actions to reflect repentance and turning away from sin, but also for our hearts to be in alignment.

When our hearts are aligned with the Lord, our thoughts and deeds will follow suit. We must seek God's help in making our outward lives a true reflection of the transformation within our hearts.

Matthew 4:16

Jesus is often described as a beacon of light. This is because His light illuminates everything, exposing its true nature. The devil wants to prevent you from discovering this truth.

The longer he can keep you in the dark, the longer he can wage war against your soul and the Kingdom of God. He understands that once you step into the light of Christ, you will uncover the truth and the authority you possess, driving him and his demons away and breaking all the chains they once used to control you.

Satan is aware that when you allow God's light to shine within you and your life, there is no place left for him, and that light will begin to drive him out of the lives of all those you hold dear, because what is yours, belongs to God as well, and what you cherish, God cherishes.

Your prayers also become a potent weapon that thwarts the devil's schemes against you and your loved ones. We are all living, breathing reflections of the Lord's divine light, spreading healing into a dying world.

September 24

Proverbs 20:19

Unfortunately, there will always be people in the world who are two-faced. I'm certain you understand what I am referring to - individuals who wear a smile when in your presence, but then spread gossip about you behind your back, tarnishing your reputation.

This passage clearly advises us to steer clear of such people. Through my experiences, I have come to realize that those who freely share others' private matters with me are likely to do the same with my own. It has been a tough lesson to learn over the years, but I have finally learned my lesson.

This has also helped me to become a better friend and confidant, as I know what it feels like to be the subject of negative gossip. If our words are causing harm to others, then we are not living right. Even if we do not particularly like someone, and even if they are unkind to us, it does not give us the right to be hateful.

As followers of Christ, we should not speak hate into the world. Instead, we should choose to speak life and love, even towards our enemies, just as Jesus did.

Exodus 20:13

Life is a valuable blessing. Each of us was created by God with the utmost love and care in His own image. When God created us, He instilled His own essence within us, along with His aspirations, dreams, and purpose.

God never intended for us to hold hatred in our hearts and harm one another. God values love, life and relationship above all else. Jesus Himself is the embodiment of love, life and relationship.

I often reflect on how Jesus, even in the midst of His suffering during His crucifixion, chose to pray for those involved and asked God to forgive them. Instead of calling upon His Father and the warrior angels in Heaven to fight against those who were causing Him harm, Jesus opted to show love, pray, and forgive.

These are the same steps we should follow when we feel hatred creeping into our hearts. Love is always the right choice and the only solution.

September 26

Numbers 6:24-26

What a wonderful way to experience peace in the presence of God, and what a sincere prayer to declare over someone's life. There is no safer place to place our trust, and the trust of our loved ones, than in the hands of our compassionate God.

With Him, there is a peace that surpasses all understanding, hope that surpasses all doubt, and confidence that surpasses all fear. In God, there is tender mercy, boundless love, and immeasurable grace. He illuminates us with His radiant light, dispelling all darkness from our lives, and making everything new and pure as it was intended to be.

I can sense the tenderness of His loving heart in this scripture, as well as His awe-inspiring power, and His willingness to listen to our prayers with the utmost affection and attention. We serve a magnificent God who loves us deeply.

I encourage you to speak this prayer over someone's life today, and every day, especially in person so they can hear this blessing being spoken over their lives. Perhaps they will then speak that blessing over someone else's life, and together we can create a chain of healing, sending out waves of love, breaking the chains of darkness all around us.

September 27

Ezra 9:6

I will always remember the day I made the decision to approach God, tears streaming down my face, trembling with repentance, fully aware of my sins against Him, others, and myself.

After reading the Bible for some time, everything hit me at once. I had made some serious mistakes. I felt unworthy of forgiveness, but I knew God offered it to me anyway.

It was difficult to grasp, and even more humbling to ask for His forgiveness. Yet, in His mercy, God offered it to me without hesitation. I accepted it eagerly, like a hungry child receiving a delicious piece of pie, relishing every bite and feeling the nourishment spread through me.

We all sin and fall short of God's glory, and no sin is greater than another - a sin is a sin. However, the Lord is always ready to welcome us back through His grace, and into His ever-loving arms.

Psalms 29:11

When faced with difficult times or a series of unfortunate events, people often wonder how you manage to stay strong and keep going. The answer to this question is simple: Jesus.

It is through the grace and strength provided by our Lord and Savior Jesus Christ that we are able to endure and overcome challenges. By sharing this with others, we have the opportunity to testify to the transformative power of our faith in Jesus.

We can explain how our trust in Him brings a peace that surpasses understanding and how God works all things for the good of those who believe in Him.

Our lives become a living example of the power of God, serving as a beacon of hope and inspiration to those around us.

This can spark curiosity in others about how to find the same peace and confidence in their own lives, and we should always be ready to point them to Jesus Christ - the Way, the Truth, and the Life.

September 29

Isaiah 35:4

We can take comfort in knowing that God is always with us, guiding us through the storms of life. His love and grace are unchanging, and His power is unmatched. We can trust in His faithfulness and lean on His strength when we feel weak. In times of uncertainty, we can find peace in His presence and assurance in His promises.

As we navigate through the chaos of the world, we can rest in the knowledge that God is in control. He is working all things together for our good, and His plans for us are always for our welfare and not for harm. We can find hope in His sovereignty and find courage in His protection.

In the face of adversity, we can stand firm in our faith, knowing that God will bring justice and righteousness. We can take comfort in the fact that He will bring about redemption and restoration for His people. We can trust in His ultimate victory over evil and His triumph over all that seeks to harm us.

So, let us hold fast to our faith and trust in the unwavering love and power of our God. In Him, we find strength, peace, and hope, even in the midst of chaos. With God by our side, we can face the unknown with confidence, knowing that He is our rock and our fortress.

Jonah 3:10

Warning signs are all around us, indicating the consequences of straying from the path that God has laid out for us. God's way is always the best way, as He desires what is best for His children as a loving Father.

The Bible contains numerous stories of individuals who faced the repercussions of their own choices. The world is in turmoil due to the sins of Adam and Eve, as well as our collective poor decisions. Without Jesus, there would be no hope of redemption.

However, God is merciful and can prevent the destruction we are heading towards if we turn our hearts to Him and sincerely repent. By leaving behind sin and embracing God's will, we can thrive in His blessings.

Just like a caring parent, God wants us to succeed and make the most of the opportunities He provides. We must face each day with determination, knowing that God is in control and will guide us through life's challenges.

October

October 1

John 6:35

There exists a void and a sense of despair in this world that only Jesus Christ can alleviate. He calls Himself the Bread of Life because He understands that He is the sole provider of sustenance that endures.

While we may attempt to fill the gaps in our lives with relationships, possessions, or busyness, none of these can truly satisfy our deepest desires. They can merely offer fleeting, incomplete contentment at best.

Jesus extends Himself to us as nourishment, freely available for us to partake in so that we may be fully satisfied. His teachings provide us with daily sustenance, offering comfort, hope, and the ability to heal the empty and shadowy corners within us.

The devil's initial act was sowing the seed of doubt, aiming to instill uncertainty in humanity regarding God's word, and he has been watering that seed ever since.

The only way to destroy what the devil has planted is to completely uproot it through unwavering faith in our Savior Jesus Christ, and to consistently nurture the seed of faith that has been planted within us.

Romans 6:6

When we accept Jesus Christ as our Savior, we are reborn in His image, shedding our old ways and embracing a new life filled with grace and redemption. As we delve deeper into the teachings of the Bible, we find guidance and wisdom to navigate the challenges of life with faith and courage.

Our relationship with God becomes the cornerstone of our existence, shaping our thoughts, words, and actions in alignment with His will. The transformation that takes place within us is evident to those around us, drawing them closer to the light of Christ through our example. We become beacons of hope and love, sharing the good news of salvation with all who are willing to listen.

As we walk in the footsteps of Jesus, we are guided by His light and truth, leading us to a life of purpose and fulfillment. The journey may be challenging at times, but we can find strength and perseverance in our faith, knowing that God is always by our side, leaving behind the darkness of our past and embracing the promise of a new beginning in Christ.

Ephesians 6:12

The devil and his legion of demons are tirelessly working against you, aware of the limited time they have to wreak havoc in the world and prevent souls from entering Heaven.

They thrive on misery and are highly skilled at creating distractions and weapons to lead you astray. The battle begins in the spiritual realm, with physical manifestations following suit.

Your adversary does not want your family to be healed, for you to release the burden of guilt, to conquer your addictions, or to realize the power you possess through God's grace to defeat him.

By putting on the armor of God each day, we make ourselves impervious to Satan and his minions. When we resist the devil, he will not just retreat, but flee in fear, knowing he cannot stand against Jesus in our lives, and that his fate is already sealed.

Acts 22:16

When we call upon the name of Jesus and accept Him as our Savior, all our sins are washed away. It is this act that cleanses us of our sins for whoever calls on the name of the Lord will be saved. Baptism is an intimate outward expression of our death and burial to a life of sin by being submerged under water, a representation of our sins being washed away, and resurrection into our new life as we rise out of the water.

It is a formal, outward declaration that we have given our lives over to the Lord in faith. Jesus Himself was baptized, and if we are meant to follow His footsteps then we should also make our way to the water to be baptized. If this is something you haven't done yet, don't wait. Reach out to your church and get a date set.

I remember the day I was baptized. Several other women and I lined up with the congregation gathered all around us, and one by one we stepped into the water as the pastor spoke of us being resurrected in the likeness of Christ. You could feel the power of the Lord and angels gathered round. The feeling was indescribable, as tears of joy, hope, and gratitude filled the hearts and eyes of all of us, and Heaven celebrated.

October 5

Luke 12:8

While I was living a life of sin, my loved ones hoped for better choices from me. They prayed for me, and eventually, God answered their prayers. It wasn't exactly how they expected, but it happened. He caught my attention, and I made the decision to surrender my life to Him.

Over the years, as I've grown closer to the Lord, my heart has opened up more to Him, becoming filled with His love. I desire for others to experience His love just as I have.

Life continues to throw challenges my way, but my perspective on handling them has shifted. I am eager to share about God and His grace with anyone willing to listen, and I enjoy hearing others' stories of their encounters with Him.

While I have faced opposition in declaring Jesus Christ as the Lord of my life, especially in public settings, I am determined to not keep this blessing to myself.

Good things are meant to be shared, and I pray that all will come to know Him, by connecting with others, sharing our faith journeys, and spreading the good news that leads to salvation.

October 6

Isaiah 41:10

Waking up and confronting the uncertainties of the day can be quite a challenge. It may be riddled with daunting obstacles such as relationship issues, financial struggles, health concerns, work problems, and a myriad of other things. Life has a way of throwing unexpected challenges our way, but we do not have to face them alone. God has promised to be with us, so there is no need to be afraid. He will see us through with His comfort, strength, and provision.

Whenever you feel alone, simply close your eyes, take a deep breath, call on His name, and envision Him holding you close, gazing at you with love and affection. There is nothing to fear, for God has a plan, and His plans for our lives are always greater than our own. Sometimes good things fall apart so that the best things can enter our lives.

Hindsight is always 20/20, but if we keep our focus on the Lord instead of the unknown journey ahead, our vision will be clear. Take a moment today to recognize and embrace His presence all around you. Appreciate the blue of the sky, the fragrance of a flower, the birds singing outside your window, and express gratitude to our loving Creator as you bask in the warmth of His love.

October 7

Psalms 100:4

There is always a reason to express gratitude. Some days, it may be effortless to be thankful, while on other days, we may need to consciously approach the Lord with a grateful attitude. By focusing on the blessings we have instead of what we lack, we can live a life of contentment with the provisions the Lord has given us.

God has promised to meet our needs, and He has not failed us this far. However, this does not mean we can be passive and expect everything to be handed to us. We still need to do our part, but God goes above and beyond to ensure that we are loved and provided for; we just need to adjust our perspective at times.

Our conversations with God and our prayers reflect our hearts, so we can assess what is stored in our hearts by reflecting on our approach to God and the words we speak to Him. Are our prayers self-centered, or do we express gratitude for helping us through difficult and frightening times? Are we praying for others? Let us take the time today to give thanks to our Creator, who extends grace to us and calls us His own.

October 8

1 Chronicles 21:13

After committing the crime that led me to prison, I exercised my Miranda Rights and opted not to engage with law enforcement. Instead of sharing my story and placing my fate in their hands, I chose to remain silent. I spent my time behind bars, entrusting my fate to the Lord.

Despite facing false accusations from others, I found peace in the knowledge that God knew the truth, and that was good enough for me. I sought forgiveness for my role in the events that brought me to that point, praying for divine judgement based on righteousness and mercy, and my prayers were answered.

Although I was looking at a lengthy prison sentence, just before my court appearance, the prosecutor proposed a plea deal of eight years. It was an answered prayer. I knew I had to face the consequences of my actions, but I also knew that God was in control.

I felt God's presence as I poured out my heart to Him, seeking forgiveness and a fresh start through His grace. He granted me that new beginning, and I haven't turned away from Him since. God's power, sovereignty, righteousness, and mercy are incredibly awesome!

Proverbs 3:1-2

As we navigate the ups and downs of life, we gather a wealth of knowledge and insight that can be passed down to future generations.

I remember the stories my grandparents shared with me about their own struggles and triumphs, and how those lessons shaped my own journey.

Now, as I grow older, I find myself imparting those same teachings to my own children and grandchildren, hoping to equip them with the tools they need to navigate life's challenges.

I see the value in sharing my experiences and wisdom with those around me, knowing that it can make a difference in their lives. Just as a candle lights up a dark room, I strive to be a beacon of guidance and support for those who come after me.

I believe that by passing on our knowledge and wisdom, we can create a ripple effect of healing and growth that will bless generations to come.

Matthew 4:21-22

When Jesus calls us, we must respond to His call with joy and faith, just as His followers in this scripture did. In this passage, His followers literally abandoned everything immediately to follow Him.

They made the decision to leave behind their old lives and even their families to follow their Lord. They sacrificed their own plans to embrace the plans of Jesus. It must have been both thrilling and frightening for them.

Their actions demonstrated their trust and dedication. They didn't say to Jesus, "I have some unfinished business here, I'll catch up with you later," or, "my family needs me right now, it's not a good time." Jesus called them, they left everything behind, and chose to follow Him.

Jesus not only calls us to salvation, but He also calls us to a purposeful life, with a series of purposes to fulfill each day. I can only hope and pray that we respond to His every call with the same faith-filled attitude as His followers did in this passage.

October 11

John 15:4

All relationships need affection, dedication, and attention for them to thrive. If we neglect relationships with those we care about, our relationships eventually wither away.

The same principle applies to our relationship with Jesus Christ. That's why it's so important for us to remain connected to Him by feeding on His word and applying it in our lives.

This is how we grow, allowing Him to work through us and bear fruit in our lives. We must firmly anchor our faith in the fertile ground of God's word to enrich our spiritual relationship with Him.

He is the source of life, and without Him, we cannot flourish. Rejecting God will only lead to unfulfilling lives. We must cling to Jesus in faith, acknowledging that we are redeemed by His blood, and that only He can provide the nourishment we need through His boundless grace.

October 12

Psalms 6:4

Feel free to pour out your heart to God and be completely honest about your struggles. He already knows everything, and He is patiently waiting for you to talk to Him.

God is the one who can handle the truth, having seen us at our lowest points and still giving us His best. Remember, nothing can separate you from His love, and He is willing to step in and help if you ask Him to.

Let Him fight your battles and share in His victories. God never turns away from us; it is us who sometimes turn away from Him. He will always fight for your love, choosing you without any doubt or hesitation.

So, if there's anything you haven't shared with your loving Father, or any situation you haven't invited Him into, take a moment to have a heartfelt conversation with Him. He is eagerly waiting to listen and ready to respond.

October 13

Exodus 20:3

Marriage is a sacred commitment between two individuals to love each other unconditionally and remain loyal through any challenges, always putting the other person's needs above their own.

Infidelity has no place in a marriage, as it contradicts the very essence of this promise. Just as God expects us to be faithful to Him after accepting us back despite our past mistakes, He wants us to put Him above all else.

He craves our complete attention and dedication, not to be pushed aside or treated as an afterthought. He yearns for us, knowing that we will never find anything or anyone else that loves us the way He does.

He doesn't want us to waste our time and effort on trivial pursuits like chasing material possessions or prioritizing someone else, or a job over Him in our lives. God's love is unmatched, and He should be the primary focus of our hearts and lives.

October 14

Leviticus 19:18

Reflect on the various ways in which you demonstrate self-love. As children of God, it's important to view ourselves and others with love, showing patience, kindness, forgiveness, and understanding. Meeting our own needs is essential, but we must also strive to meet the needs of others.

Just as God freely offers grace, we should extend the same grace to ourselves and those around us. We are all part of one big family sharing this planet, so let us make the most of our time here until we are called to our eternal home.

Each of us has strengths, weaknesses, and unique gifts that are valuable to God and beneficial in serving His Kingdom. Loving others is a way of expressing holiness, prioritizing love over self.

Love always seeks to improve the world, even in challenging circumstances. By reflecting the image of Christ, we can break free from the chains that the devil has placed in our lives.

Take a moment today to show love and care to those around you, seizing every opportunity to make a positive impact.

October 15

2 Samuel 22:17-20

As children of God, we may be spared from certain trials in life, but we will undoubtedly encounter many others. While God assures us that He will guide us through every challenge, He never guarantees that we won't have to struggle.

God's love for His children is boundless, and He uses life's trials to shape our character and bring us closer to Him. These trials serve to reveal more about God's nature and our own.

Whether we are up against a seemingly insurmountable foe - be it a person, a group, a health issue, or an addiction - we are never alone in the battle. Your Savior is alive and fighting alongside you through whatever you are facing.

He will deliver you because of His deep love for you, even if it may not happen in the way we expect. All you need is faith as small as a mustard seed to move the mountain in front of you; God will handle the heavy lifting; all you need to do is have faith.

1 Kings 8:56

I'm not sure about you, but I tend to be quite impatient when it comes to getting what I want. It's a daily struggle for me to work on being patient. I have a hard time sitting still and always want to rush things, even though it often ends up slowing things down or causing problems. However, I am learning!

By reading God's word and reflecting on His promises for my life, I can see how He brings them to fruition in His perfect timing and in His own way, especially when I step back and let Him work.

God's promises never fail, regardless of how many times we may fail ourselves, or others may fail us. While we may experience sorrow for a time, joy always comes in the morning! Don't let what you see today make you doubt what the Lord has in store for you tomorrow. When God speaks, it is already done. His words are fulfilled the moment He utters them.

I encourage you to dive into God's word today and remind yourself of all the wonderful promises He has made for your life. Let the truth of His word drown out the lies of the world.

October 17

Psalms 19:14

Consider the impact of the words you speak each day. Are you using a lot of profanity? Speaking negatively about others? Speaking negatively about yourself?

The words that come out of your mouth reflect what is in your heart. If God were to examine your heart and listen to your words today, what would He discover?

The truth is, He is paying attention. Would He be pleased? Or would He encourage you to make better choices?

We know that words hold power. They can alter the course of any situation, change minds, provide healing and hope, or cause harm. It all stems from what is stored in our hearts.

If you feel that your words need improvement, turn to the Lord in prayer and seek His guidance. Dive into His word and let it cleanse your heart. Remember, the impact of your words can be far-reaching, so choose them wisely.

October 18

Jeremiah 15:19

This scripture encourages those who have devoted themselves to serving the Lord to approach Him with a repentant heart, seeking forgiveness for their mistakes. It emphasizes the importance of avoiding sin and following God's will in every aspect of life.

Moreover, it underscores the responsibility that comes with serving God. As His representatives, our words and actions should mirror His presence in our lives.

Some may be drawn to us, while others may oppose us. In the face of opposition, it’s vital to remain steadfast in our beliefs and values, unwavering in our faith.

Ultimately, this scripture highlights the qualities that God values in His servants: sincerity, courage, and faithfulness. It urges us to fulfill His will with dedication and perseverance until the end. By adhering to these principles, we can honor and serve the Lord in a manner that pleases Him.

Daniel 9:23

Prayer is significant. Just take a look at how many situations in the Bible were transformed because someone prayed to God. When we send up a prayer to God, it's like calling 911 for our lives. Things start to change, even if we can't see it at first, and God begins to send His reinforcements to work in our situation.

When we pray, our prayers go straight to the top of the chain of the army of God, and He starts giving out the orders. We are so special to God that we don't have to go through the hoops of a worldly command system; we get to have direct access to Him at all times, anywhere, no matter what. Isn't that amazing?

All of our prayers are important to God, but we should also think about how we pray. Are we passionate in our prayers, devoted to the Lord, not only asking for our heart's desires, but also considering His? Are we using prayer time as a way to come to know and love Him better? Is God your go-to in all circumstances?

God listens to your prayers because He loves you and wants an intimate relationship with you, and if you listen closely, He will share His hopes and dreams with you too.

October 20

Ezekiel 33:11

When God saw us at our lowest, He didn't say, "they are beyond saving. I give up." Instead, He fought with even greater determination. He graciously sent His beloved son to offer us a chance to come back to Him.

He built a fireproof bridge after we burned down the old one. He does not desire for us to die in our sins, yet He respects our free will. I earnestly pray for those who deny God's existence and for those who claim to believe but live contrary to His ways.

I am not referring to occasional mistakes, but to those who consistently prioritize their own desires, pursuing money, pleasure, violence, or power while disregarding God and expecting blessings.

Even if they achieve their goals, we know that only God's children will enter Heaven when this life ends. Let us persist in praying for the lost to be guided back, so they may abandon selfishness and find peace in the Lord's loving arms.

Luke 9:25

Before accepting Jesus as my Lord and Savior, I recall my previous mindset and the pursuits I engaged in. I was focused on my own desires, relentlessly pursuing whatever it was that I wanted at the time. If anyone stood in my way, I would go to great lengths to remove them. I was indifferent to the consequences of my poor decisions, as long as I got what I wanted when I wanted it.

Reflecting on my selfishness pains me. While I cannot undo the mistakes I have made, I strive to live each day in a way that honors God. I aim to show love and kindness towards those I hold dear, always mindful of how my actions reflect God and impact those around me.

We only have one life to make each moment count, and we don't know how many moments remain. Therefore, why not use these moments to honor our Creator and Savior, allowing the Holy Spirit to guide us in spreading salvation to others before it is too late. The only pursuit worth undertaking in this life is Jesus.

October 22

John 3:18

This passage brings either great comfort or profound sorrow. It provides peace to those who have faith, love, trust, and devotion to Jesus Christ, yet my heart aches for those who do not.

We know that we are no longer under condemnation, but under God's grace now that we are saved, while those who do not believe are still condemned. Our past sins are forgiven by God once the blood of Jesus cleanses us.

However, there are those in the world who are still burdened by the weight of their sins, either by choice or due to not being told of the cleansing power available to them. This is why it’s crucial for us to spread the message of salvation.

Belief in the Son of God is the only way into Heaven. The day of God's final judgement is approaching, and we all must make a decision about where we wish to spend eternity. Sin created a divide between us and God, but Jesus has the ability to absolve us of all our sins and reunite us with our Heavenly Father; all we need to do is have faith.

October 23

Romans 15:13

The simple pleasures in life bring me a lot of happiness - the laughter of my children, the warmth of a hug from my grandchildren, and the comfort of a home-cooked meal shared with loved ones. These moments fill my heart with joy and gratitude, reminding me of the abundance of blessings in my life.

But when challenges arise and financial struggles loom, I turn to my faith for strength and guidance. I trust in God's plan for me, knowing that He will provide for my needs and lead me through difficult times. In moments of uncertainty, I find comfort in prayer and meditation, seeking His peace and wisdom to navigate the storms of life.

Through it all, I am grateful for the unwavering love and support of my unfailing Savior, who stands by me in times of need. His presence is a constant source of comfort and encouragement, reminding me that I am never alone on my journey.

And as I continue to walk in faith and gratitude, I am filled with hope for the future, knowing that God's grace will always guide me towards a brighter tomorrow.

October 24

1 Chronicles 16:11

I am inherently prone to worrying, as past experiences have conditioned my mind to anticipate the worst-case scenarios. This habit has allowed me to feel a sense of control and readiness for whatever challenges life may bring.

Through divine intervention, God has guided me away from this negative cycle of thinking, redirecting my focus towards His presence. Although it has been a gradual process, I have reached a point where, in times of difficulty, I remind myself to look up and trust in Him.

I no longer need to be consumed by anxiety over the uncertainties of the future, as I have the Lord by my side, undefeated in every battle. Victory may not always appear as expected, just as the crucifixion of Jesus did not seem like a victory at first glance, yet it undeniably was.

True strength is found in drawing near to God and fixing our gaze upon Him. While perfection is not demanded of us, God will refine us as we courageously face each new day, responding to His call and remaining steadfast in our faith.

October 25

Nehemiah 9:5-6

When you gaze out the window at night, the sky is filled with countless stars illuminating the darkness.

Strolling along the beach, you witness the vastness of the ocean stretching endlessly before you, feeling the sand between your toes.

And when you envision the one you hold dearest in your heart, remember that all these wonders share a common thread. They were all intricately crafted by our magnificent Creator.

Every beautiful sight, every delightful sensation, every heartfelt emotion - all gifts from our loving Father. He deserves not just a little praise, but endless adoration.

Just as we appreciate recognition for our efforts, God too deserves our genuine and sincere praise. Make it a habit to praise Him in the morning, during the day, and before you go to sleep, and watch how your soul is nourished with each act of devotion.

Jonah 2:1-2

Jonah realized he had made a mistake. He attempted to escape from God and went against His message, but even while he was inside the belly of the whale, he recognized the compassionate nature of God and prayed to Him. God's nature remains unchanged; He is still a caring, merciful Father who readily extends compassion even when we are at our lowest.

Even when we are enduring the severe consequences of our sins, God is waiting for us to cry out, humbly admit our disobedience, and turn away from our sinful ways. God hears our pleas, and through His grace, He responds to them. There is no one else we can depend on to be with us in every circumstance. The Lord is the only one who truly understands the depth of the messes we find ourselves in and knows how to guide us through and out of them.

Salvation comes solely from the Lord. Therefore, when you realize that you have strayed from the path set by God, do not hesitate to turn to Him in prayer. He loves you unconditionally. And if you are unsure of what to pray, remember that the Spirit helps us in our weakness and intercedes for us in the midst of our suffering.

October 27

John 3:16

As a parent, you can probably imagine how it must have felt for God to send His only beloved son into the world to endure a painful death in order to save it. Not only that, but His son was completely innocent.

Both God and Jesus knew the outcome, but their love for us made the sacrifice worth it. They knew that the temporary suffering would lead to eternal glory.

Their sacrifice ensures that our lives don't end when our bodies do. Take a moment to fully understand how much you are loved by the Creator. If you ever doubt your worth, remember that Jesus died for YOU!

You are incredibly valuable to God. Memorize this verse and repeat it whenever you feel down on yourself. You are priceless! God has invested His own blood and life into you, His beloved, because of His immense love for you. And because of this love, you will spend eternity in Heaven with Love Himself.

Romans 14:7-9

Our lives are not defined by our circumstances, but by the presence and grace of God. Jesus didn't just come to earth to sacrifice Himself for us, but He also rose from the dead and defeated death itself to become the Lord of both the living and the dead. We are His in this life and the next.

Therefore, we must live our lives with purpose, knowing that we are no longer living for ourselves, but for the Lord. There will come a time when we will also lay down our lives for Him. Our lives and the decisions we make impact not only those around us, but also future generations.

We can leave behind a legacy of healing or destruction, life or death. Jesus demonstrated the difference that one life, one person can make, and the lasting effects of His presence, choices, and influence.

His power resides within you, and the consequences of your choices will shape history in ways you may not realize. I urge you to be mindful of your words and actions today, and consider the impact you are making on the world. Are you spreading life or death?

Zechariah 10:11-12

As we pass through the sea of trouble, it can be easy to feel overwhelmed and defeated. But as believers, we have the assurance that we are not alone in our struggles. God is always with us, ready to provide us with the strength and guidance we need to navigate through difficult times.

The Holy Spirit serves as our constant companion, leading us in the right direction and offering us peace and wisdom. With God by our side, we can face any obstacle with confidence, knowing that He has a plan for our lives and will never abandon us.

Even in our moments of weakness and despair, we can find comfort in the knowledge that God's love for us is unwavering. His compassion knows no bounds, and He is always ready to extend His grace and mercy to us.

Through prayer, faith, and a deepening relationship with God, we can tap into the limitless power and resources available to us as His children. So let us take comfort in the fact that we serve a God who is faithful and true, and who will never leave us nor forsake us.

Psalms 16:11

Embrace the fact that as a beloved child of God, you are destined to experience a life filled with increasing glory. Your current situation is a stark contrast to your past, as God's radiance shines through you, illuminating every aspect of your life from the spiritual realm to the physical world.

Just like the morning sun that grows brighter until noon, the righteous path you walk on leads to greater light. The Holy Spirit guides us, filling us with His presence and steering us towards our divine purpose.

By finding joy in God's presence rather than worldly pleasures, we can experience fulfillment in knowing our loving Creator and anticipating an eternity in Heaven.

When we cherish our relationship with God and live according to His will, we break free from the chains of sin that once bound us. Embracing Christ transforms us, and in the process, transforms everything around us.

2 Samuel 22:7

There are moments when we may question if God is listening to our prayers. We might have been asking and pleading with Him for a long time, but it feels like He is not responding.

We need to remember that God does hear us, regardless of how we feel. It is not based on our emotions, but on His promise.

He has heard every tear we've shed, every sigh of our hearts, and every desperate plea we've made. Psalm 139:4 NIV says, "Before a word is on my tongue you, Lord, know it completely."

He knows everything about us, and our prayers have direct access to Him. We are precious to Him, and He cares deeply about what we are going through.

We need to trust Him, even in the quiet times, and have faith that His answer is already on its way.

November

November 1

John 8:34

In short, this passage states that whatever we have not conquered, controls us. If we have not gained self-control over our sinful tendencies, then we are still enslaved by them. We always have a choice.

We can either let our desires dominate us, or we can allow Jesus' power to liberate us. He came to shatter chains, but unfortunately, some individuals have become comfortable with their bondage.

Jesus will not force anyone to let Him release them. The battle is not just external; it rages within us daily. Our human nature is inclined towards sin, so we must resist our fleshly desires.

The outcome of this internal struggle depends entirely on us, the weapons we wield, and who we choose to stand beside us in battle. We cannot achieve victory alone, which is why we have a Savior.

To overcome the sin that assails us, we must put on the armor of God and call upon our Savior to free us from the burdensome chains that hold us back. He has never been defeated, and He will not be defeated now!

November 2

Matthew 6:22

The way in which we perceive what we see holds great significance. It is not solely about the act of seeing, but also about the perspective from which we view things.

As we immerse ourselves in the teachings of God's word, our perception begins to align with His perspective. This alignment allows for clearer vision, enabling us to make more informed decisions regarding our approach to various situations.

A clear vision signifies walking in the truth, while a distorted vision indicates walking in darkness, potentially leading to missteps or causing others to falter. Possessing clear vision aids in distinguishing between what is godly and what is not, reflecting the condition of our hearts.

By focusing on positive aspects and goodness, our entire being becomes filled with light, and our lives radiate that light. This radiance is the presence of God Himself, turning us into beacons of His goodness wherever we go.

November 3

1 Samuel 2:2

Jesus is described as our rock in the Bible. Rocks symbolize protection, stability, and refuge. Throughout history, people sought shelter in caves, mountains, or rocky areas when faced with storms or enemies.

Jesus is our Holy rock, and there is no other rock like Him. He can withstand any storm and shut out any enemy.

We can always find refuge and stability in Him. No one is powerful enough to move Him from His place. We never have to wonder where to find Him.

The only thing the enemy can do is try to deceive us and lead us away from the rock. The enemy cannot harm Jesus, so we can find peace in knowing that He is always our safe place, our solid foundation, and our refuge in times of trouble. We can always rely on Him.

2 Kings 20:5

I still recall the time when I was eight months pregnant, battling a fever, feeling weak, and put on bedrest due to pre-eclampsia. My then husband struggled with a drug addiction that controlled our lives. He left me with no money, took our only vehicle, and I had no one to help me care for our first son who was still a toddler.

I remember sitting in the hallway, tears streaming down my face, feeling lost and unsure of what to do. I felt utterly alone, but God clearly heard my cries because my family, friends, and neighbors all came together to show their love and support, helping me get through that difficult time.

They cooked meals, brought groceries, drove me to doctor appointments, prayed for me, and looked after my son. I will always remember the love and kindness that the Lord displayed through their hearts, words, and actions.

Just before I gave birth to our second son, my husband returned home, but that marriage didn't last. God saw every tear and guided me to where I truly belonged, showering countless blessings along the way. Remember, He sees you, He understands your pain, and He is already working to bring healing into your life.

November 5

2 Chronicles 7:14

Oh, how I wish the world would embrace this scripture and take it to heart! The solution to addressing all the issues in the world is right here. And it doesn't require much.

We must all willingly acknowledge Jesus as our Lord and Savior, bearing His name, approaching Him humbly in prayer, seeking Him above all else with repentance, and turning away from our sinfulness. Then, He will forgive all our sins and heal the land.

This offer remains an open invitation for everyone even today. It is an invitation of hope and promise. However, people need to be invited to the cross in order to accept and receive this healing. Have you shared about Jesus with anyone recently? Or how to accept Him as their Savior? Are you inviting people to church?

If we desire for our land to be healed, we must be messengers, spreading His message for all to hear. And we must be consistent and persistent. Nurturing seeds that have already been sown, and sowing the seed of the gospel in new soil. This is the only way to gain ground until the day our Lord returns, and then it will be too late.

November 6

Psalms 9:7

The truth is the truth, no matter who believes it. God reigns as the Supreme Authority over all of creation, with no equal.

This reality holds true even for those who do not believe, yet for believers, there is comfort in knowing that our loving and just God governs us.

We can offer praise to His name for His constant presence and unwavering support. God's victory is absolute, and we can rejoice in this victory both in the present and in the afterlife.

Our Creator is mighty to save, merciful in forgiveness, patient in longsuffering, and righteous in His judgments. We could not ask for a better God. He is divine, perfect, and Holy.

The world and everything in it will pass away, but the name of the Lord will endure for eternity, and with His name, so shall we endure because we bear His name.

Proverbs 14:9

If someone who knows us well is asked about us, "what is he/she like?" What do you think their response would be? They would probably respond with something to do with our character. They might say, "he/she is kind, funny, helpful, a hard worker, a devout Christian," or they could say, "he/she is lazy, mean, doesn't like to be bothered, doesn't believe in God, etc."

Our character boils down to us either caring about others, or not caring about others. We can either choose to live upright by way of virtue, caring for our brothers and sisters in Christ, or we can choose to act as fools mocking them.

Fools always have an excuse and go their own way, while the upright do their best to make wise choices, own their wrongs, and care about the feelings of others. It all comes down to our attitudes and the condition of our hearts.

All of our choices will be brought into account in the end, so, we simply have to ask ourselves at the end of the day if our conscience is clean, and if not-what can we do tomorrow to make it right?

Zechariah 7:9-10

Jesus took to the streets to attend to the needs of others. He provided food for the hungry, healed the sick and dying, and shared the good news of God. It is important for us to emulate His actions by showing kindness and mercy to those who are in desperate need.

The world can be harsh, but Jesus used His position, resources, and even His own life to save others, and we are called to do the same. We must come together, forgive one another, and avoid holding hatred in our hearts towards others. We should hate the sin but love the sinner.

While it may be easy to show kindness and compassion to those we know and care for, we must also extend it to strangers and even our enemies. We were once enemies of God, yet He still showed us grace and paid the price for our sins.

Look for opportunities to show kindness to someone today, especially to those who may not be known for their kindness and allow the love of God to work through you to break the chains of indifference in your life and the lives of those around you.

November 9

John 6:63

The Spirit is the sole source of life within us. Human endeavors are useless. The word of God breathes life into all aspects of our lives that are dying or dead.

In order for us to be nourished by it, we must consume it. It serves as the sustenance for our lives.

We may attempt to take control of the steering wheel, and steer the vehicle in any direction we choose, towards the destination we desire, but without fuel in the tank, we won't make it very far.

We cannot simultaneously push and steer the vehicle, and even if we could, our energy would quickly run out. When our lives fall apart, Jesus is the glue that puts us back together.

We can pursue life and allow the Spirit to heal us by embracing the word of God with obedience and faith, bringing honor to His name, the name above all names.

November 10

Romans 12:12

The world may seem bleak at times, but as Christians, we have a hopeful outlook. We can find joy in looking beyond what is visible to us and focusing on what God has planned for our future. Our current struggles are temporary.

Jesus warned us about facing challenges, but also reassured us that He has already conquered them. When difficulties arise, we can navigate through them with patience by changing our perspective, understanding that each trial we endure helps shape our character and strength as we journey towards Heaven.

Through constant prayer and connection with God, we have access to peace, comfort, guidance, protection, and provision to help us overcome any obstacles. Though we live in this world, we are not defined by it. By relying on the cleansing power of Jesus Christ, we can conquer the world and all its challenges.

November 11

1 Corinthians 1:7

Each of us has been blessed by God with spiritual gifts that are essential for fulfilling the purposes He has designed for us. He ensures that we have everything we need to carry out our mission in Christ.

As we work together, we form the body of Christ, reaching out across the world to spread healing and light. It takes teamwork to make the dream work!

If you are uncertain about your gifts, seek guidance from your fellow believers and pray for the Lord to reveal them to you and guide you on the path He has planned for you. We must embrace the unique gifts that we have been given. These gifts are not of our choosing; they are bestowed upon us by God's design and grace.

We all have abilities; we simply need to allow God to use them and work through us so that we may bring glory to our Heavenly Father and honor the sacrifice of Jesus. As Christians, we have been set apart to do good works. We have been blessed with privilege, hope, and the power to overcome the enemy through love.

November 12

Mark 9:23

We can all connect with this in our lives. As children of God, we have faith in the Lord, but we also strive to grow in our faith to overcome our shortcomings. We all face challenges with our faith at times.

When I started mentoring and ministering to recovering addicts and those in prison, I was full of zeal! I was on a mission to save lives and souls, and I knew the Lord was with me. Over time, I was able to help many people accept Jesus Christ as their Savior, and there's nothing more rewarding than being part of that process.

However, I couldn't save everyone. Some returned to their old ways, and others lost their lives. Witnessing these events started to steal my joy and I began to feel defeated. So, I prayed. Hard. And God continued to guide me on the path He had set for me, but He refined me in the process.

I had to realize that I can't save everyone, but I can lead them to the one who can, and the choice is up to them after that. Even when we are unsure of ourselves, there is no doubt about who God is. Pray today for the Lord to help you trust Him so that you may be strengthened in your faith as you do His work.

Psalms 19:12-13

I regularly pray for myself, my children, and grandchildren. Sin is a reality, and temptation is a powerful tool of the enemy.

Often, we are unaware of our own faults, requiring those close to us to point them out. David sought God's forgiveness for his unknown sins and asked for strength to resist intentional wrongdoing.

Sin and temptation may not always be obvious, often creeping in slowly. It is crucial to remain vigilant and exercise self-control to avoid falling into temptation.

In my prayers, I also ask God to remove any obstacles that may lead us astray and to bring into our lives those who will guide us closer to Him.

While the consequence of sin is death, we have been given the gift of eternal life through Jesus Christ. Let us not return to our past chains but embrace the freedom that comes with our Salvation.

November 14

Deuteronomy 20:4

I used to avoid public speaking at all costs until I felt called by the Lord to do it occasionally. It wasn't something I felt confident in.

After getting to know Jesus and reading God's word, I remembered when God called Moses to speak, and Moses made excuses about not being good with words.

Even though God allowed Moses' brother to speak for him, Moses focused on his shortcomings instead of God's power. Letting fear and doubt control us can cause us to miss out on blessings and opportunities.

So, when God presents a chance to bring Him glory, I always accept. I show up and trust God to handle the rest. I may be nervous and lose sleep the night before, but with each victory the Lord gives me, I gain ground.

There are times I wish I had done better, but every experience is a win, and I'm learning and enjoying God's presence. It's not just about the journey, but also about who is with you along the way.

November 15

1 Kings 8:58

Our bodies are sacred places for God, and we should strive to make Him feel at home like gracious hosts. He resides in our hearts, bodies, minds, and lives as we open our doors to Him.

When we ask for His guidance and strength to stay true to Him, we acknowledge our tendency to wander, helping us to keep unwelcome guests out of our lives.

True devotion in any relationship means respecting and caring for the other person's boundaries, feelings, and wishes. Our actions, or lack thereof, reflect how we feel about the other person.

And to the next generations who are watching, we are passing on these values or lack of values to them.

Therefore, we must do our best to welcome the Lord into our lives and become comfortable with Him taking control of the things we have neglected. We need to learn to follow His lead and guidance as He renews and transforms us.

November 16

Romans 8:18

The idea that suffering can actually strengthen our hope may seem strange, but that is precisely what this scripture implies.

Suffering entails some form of pain, and when we are in pain, it is challenging for that not to become our focal point.

As believers, we have hope to help and see us through our suffering. We have the assurance of God's word and the hope of future glory in Heaven where suffering does not exist.

We can triumph over any suffering we may face at present by recognizing that it only brings us closer to God, and the devil's attempts to use it to drive us away from God will not succeed.

We have, and will always have, the victory, living from glory to glory until the day of Jesus Christ's return.

A place in Heaven awaits us with our names written on it, and we cannot even begin to imagine the blessings and peace that await us.

November 17

Zephaniah 2:3

I have experienced the wrath of many people, but I have always managed to stand up again. However, I understand that those who face God's wrath will not have the same chance. We can endure the devil's attacks and walk away, but we cannot escape the final blow from the Lord.

The thought of God being so angry pains me, and I can only imagine how much it hurts Him to see His beloved creations turning away from Him. Our Heavenly Father does not delight in the death of the wicked; He would rather see them repent and be saved.

I desire to be as close to Jesus as possible when that day arrives, and I wish for all my loved ones to be there with me, so that God may only see Jesus in us and protect us.

I believe you share the same desire, so let us approach the Lord with humility, gratitude, and a recognition of our dependence on Him. Let us continue to seek and praise Him above all else, so that we may be shielded from His wrath on the day of judgement.

November 18

John 3:17

Jesus was sent as a message of love and forgiveness as a powerful truth that continues to inspire and guide us. His teachings on compassion, forgiveness, and selflessness have the power to transform hearts and minds, leading us to live more meaningful and fulfilling lives.

Jesus' life and example serves as a reminder that we are all beloved children of God, deserving of love and forgiveness. His willingness to sacrifice Himself for the sake of others demonstrates the depth of God's love for humanity and the lengths to which God will go to offer us redemption and salvation.

Through Jesus, we are shown that true strength comes from vulnerability and that true fulfillment comes from serving others and living in alignment with God's will.

In a world that often values power, wealth, and success, Jesus' message of love and forgiveness offers a radical alternative – one that prioritizes compassion, humility, and selflessness. His example of love and forgiveness is a powerful demonstration of the boundless grace and mercy that God offers to all who seek it, inviting us to live lives of purpose, meaning, and joy.

November 19

2 Corinthians 7:10

Grief is a necessary tool that helps us process our pain. When we experience godly grief, it leads us to repentance and salvation. However, if we choose to handle our pain in a worldly manner, we risk getting trapped in a cycle of replaying past mistakes in our minds, which only brings more pain to ourselves and those around us.

We have to acknowledge that what's done is done, and accept our mistakes, seek the grace that God offers us, make amends when possible, and move forward with the valuable lessons we have learned. By doing so, we equip ourselves with the necessary tools to prevent further sin from entering our lives, not allowing the weight of guilt to drag us down, but instead allowing the blood of Jesus to cleanse us completely.

When we genuinely love someone, we strive to avoid causing them pain. This same principle should guide us in showing our love for God. We must evaluate our choices to ensure they do not cause any pain to the Lord's heart. Guilt is like a weed that must be uprooted before it drains the life out of us, and Jesus is the Master Gardener we can turn to for help in removing it and preserving our spiritual garden.

Job 5:17-18

The term discipline always causes me to feel a bit uneasy whenever I hear it. My mind immediately associates it with an event that would likely be uncomfortable or painful in some way. And while that may be true, it doesn't necessarily mean it's a negative thing.

During my childhood, I recall my parents grounding me whenever I would disobey their rules. I absolutely hated it! The days seemed endless and dull as I eagerly awaited the day I could go back outside to play with my friends.

I also frequently had additional chores assigned to me while I endured my grounding, however, once my punishment was over, life felt good again, and I was relieved to have moved past my period of discipline.

I also became more careful in avoiding the same mistakes. I knew my parents loved me, even if I didn't enjoy facing the consequences of my actions. Similarly, we have the same assurance in knowing that when our Father in Heaven disciplines us, it is always for our benefit and is carried out with love.

November 21

Deuteronomy 32:3

The journey of faith is a remarkable one, filled with ups and downs, twists and turns. Through it all, I have experienced the incredible power of God's grace working in my life. His love has brought me through the darkest of times and lifted me up to new heights of joy and peace. I am constantly in awe of His presence and the way He orchestrates every detail of my life for my good.

I am grateful for the victories He has brought me, both big and small, and I am inspired by the transformation I see in the lives of those around me. It is a privilege to witness His hand at work, guiding and shaping us into the people He has called us to be.

As I reflect on the goodness of God, I am filled with a sense of wonder and gratitude. His faithfulness never fails, and His love knows no bounds. I am humbled by His grace and overwhelmed by His mercy. I am truly blessed to have such a loving and powerful God as my Father.

Let us continue to share the joy of His presence with the world, spreading His love and proclaiming His glory to all who will listen. May we never tire of celebrating the amazing work of our God and may we always give Him the praise and honor He deserves.

Amos 5:14

We find what we seek. It's as simple as that. We either enjoy the benefits of our pursuits, or we face the consequences. If our goal is to spend our weekends drinking and bar hopping, that's exactly what we end up doing.

We then have to deal with the inevitable hangover, with nothing to show for the money spent on alcohol, and hoping we were wise enough not to drive drunk or bring a stranger into our bed. There are many ways that situation could unfold, and none of them are worth bragging about.

Alternatively, we could choose to spend the weekend with someone we care about, getting some fresh air with good company, perhaps enjoying a nice meal, and going to church together on Sunday. No hangovers, no regrets, just happy memories and quality time spent with God.

The quality of our lives is determined by the things we pursue. When we're living right, God supports us, when we're not, God redirects us, but He always loves us. So, let's do our part to make His job and our lives a little easier, and pursue things that are approved by God.

November 23

Romans 3:23

There is no justification for sin, and our own efforts cannot absolve us of our sins. No amount of good deeds can outweigh even the smallest sin. We cannot build a pathway to Heaven on our own. However, the good news is that God has already paved the way through Jesus Christ.

Access to the Father is only possible through the son. In life, it often boils down to who you are acquainted with rather than what you know. Establishing good connections can open up new opportunities in terms of career, relationships, and other pursuits.

Knowing the right people can grant you access to circles that would otherwise be out of reach. Fortunately, Jesus Christ is always available to guide you towards the best that life and the afterlife have to offer. He is the link to all things good.

All you need to do is invite Him in and allow Him to lead the way. The blessings in our lives are not earned, but rather bestowed upon us by the grace of God, who showers us with love simply for the sake of love itself.

Matthew 11:28

When life's pressures become overwhelming, who do you rely on for support? Who is the person you turn to when you need help navigating through tough times? If you don't have someone to lean on, how do you cope with the challenges that come your way?

It's important to have a plan in place because there will be moments when we feel like we can't go on. Thankfully, there is someone we can always count on - Jesus. He is always there, never too busy or tired, and He prioritizes us above all else. Jesus is waiting for you to reach out to Him, eager to help you carry your burdens and find peace.

Some things are too heavy for us to handle alone, but our Lord and Savior is more than capable of carrying them for us once we surrender and ask for His help. If you feel like you've reached your limit, find peace in Jesus.

Trust Him with your worries and surround yourself with fellow believers who can offer support during difficult times. And when you come out of your season of struggle, be there for others in need, just as they were there for you.

November 25

Proverbs 15:3

The scripture brings a lot to the table. For believers in Jesus, it provides reassurance that God is omnipresent.

It also serves as a moral compass, reminding us that God observes our actions, whether in public or behind closed doors.

Despite the chaos in the world, God remains focused and attentive to everything, not just our lives but all of creation. It's absolutely remarkable!

Even when the wicked prosper, God sees it all. While we may witness injustice, we can take comfort in the fact that a day of judgment is coming.

The only sins that God forgets are those forgiven through Jesus. All other sins will be accounted for.

For those who are saved, there is a profound sense of love and protection in knowing that God is always watching over us. As for the wicked, it's a call to repent and return to God before it's too late.

November 26

James 5:16

When I reflect on the act of confessing my sins, I feel a sense of vulnerability. It's not easy to admit my wrongdoings to another person or to God, but I've realized that it takes courage and humility to take ownership of my mistakes.

After confessing, I always feel lighter and freer. Opening up and letting the truth shine in helps us reclaim lost ground from the devil.

God is always ready to forgive us when we sincerely confess our sins to Him. Confessing to others paves the way for healing, especially through the prayers of fellow believers.

This is why it's so important for us to support each other and gather together. Through prayer, we engage in a direct conversation with God and experience His loving, healing presence.

We can pray anytime, anywhere, knowing that He will respond in His own grace-filled way.

November 27

1 Corinthians 2:9-10

God's love for you is limitless. There will be times when we wish things were different, and there will be chapters in our lives that we wish were written differently, but this scripture gives us hope!

Instead of dwelling on our sorrows and focusing on what seems to be going wrong, let's focus on God's promises, knowing that He always keeps His word.

Let's praise Him for His presence and rely on His strength to get us through tough times, because there's not only a light at the end of the tunnel, but there's also a light with us in every moment.

God's word tells us that He has great things in store for us, we just need to trust and believe in Him. God has already revealed these things to us through His Holy Spirit and His word.

We have the assurance of Heaven and God's blessings pouring into our lives at every moment, we simply need to look up, adjust our focus, and set our minds on things above.

November 28

Mark 11:25

Forgiveness can be a beautiful concept in theory, but when it comes to actually practicing it, it can be quite challenging. It may not always be enjoyable to forgive others, even though the idea of forgiveness itself is noble.

However, holding onto grudges can lead to destructive emotions like bitterness, anxiety, and depression, as well as spiritual struggles, which can consume us and hinder our ability to receive healing and blessings.

Unforgiveness is like a poison that spreads throughout our being, affecting every aspect of our lives. Jesus emphasized the importance of forgiveness (Matthew 18:21-22), showing us that while forgiveness may not be easy, it is achievable.

By accepting the forgiveness freely given to us by the Lord, we can find the strength to extend that same forgiveness to others. When we choose to forgive those who have hurt us, we rid ourselves of the poison of unforgiveness and open the door to healing. Forgiveness is a gift that benefits both the giver and the receiver.

Luke 21:36

This passage is often misunderstood. It does not encourage us to focus on the fear-inducing news that the media promotes.

Instead, it instructs us to be vigilant about our own spiritual well-being. This message aligns perfectly with the preceding verses (Luke 21:34-35).

We need to be mindful of the choices we make in our lives. Living recklessly and following worldly desires will not lead to a positive outcome.

As stated in Matthew 24:36, "But about that day or hour no one knows, not even the angels in Heaven, nor the Son, but only the Father."

Therefore, staying informed through the news will not prepare us for the future, but nurturing our relationship with the Lord and living righteously will.

We must consistently reflect on our actions and emulate Jesus to find our way back home to our Heavenly Father.

November 30

Micah 4:5

There are numerous belief systems and religions around the world today, each with their own unique principles, traditions, deities, and rituals that shape the way their followers live their lives.

The way people conduct themselves, their actions, and their character all reflect their beliefs. Whether a person believes in a higher power or not is evident in their behavior.

Jesus' life on Earth was characterized by love, forgiveness, grace, teaching, authority, and service. He also triumphed over death.

He didn't come as a dictator barking orders and putting people in their place. Instead, He was a patient, compassionate leader, guiding us so that we could all succeed.

Our lives should mirror His example and leadership qualities to lead others to victory, as we serve the one true God, the Creator of Heaven and Earth. There is no other above Him.

December

Matthew 6:33

Oh, the joy of setting priorities! One of the phrases I often joke about is, “adulting sucks!” Making sure bills are paid, taxes are done, car maintenance is taken care of, the house is clean, meals are cooked, doctor’s appointments are scheduled, and so on, can be quite a drag. But it’s all part of being responsible.

At the end of the day, though, I feel grateful when I can check everything off my list. I see it as a blessing from God, who provides me with the means to get it all done.

The same can be said of our spiritual lives. Are we putting God first? Or are we prioritizing worldly things that bring temporary pleasure? Are we following God’s will or our own desires?

When we make God our top priority, everything falls into place. The right things will come to us, and the wrong things will fade away. This is the key to a truly fulfilling life and everlasting joy.

December 2

John 14:6

If we were to go walking through the Amazon rainforest, we would want to have a map, a guide, and supplies.

It's a dangerous place, filled with things that can harm or even kill you, and it's incredibly vast. It would be easy to get lost and never find your way out.

Life is similar in that we need a guide - Jesus, a map - the Bible, and supplies - spiritual gifts. It's the only way to navigate through.

Everything we need to make it to Heaven can only be found through our Savior Jesus Christ. Without Him, there is no hope.

Jesus is our living hope, sent to save us from everything that seeks to destroy us, and to help us find our way as we journey through the challenges of life.

He freely offers Himself to us, reaching out His hand to bring peace to our troubled hearts, and confidence as we rely on Him to lead us home.

Psalms 37:13

God is aware of all things, even the devious schemes that the wicked devise. He is not taken aback by anything.

He finds amusement in the wicked's plans because He understands that their evil actions only bring about their own downfall.

Ultimately, they are only causing harm to themselves. God always manages to bring good out of every attempt by the devil and his followers to oppose Him.

In the end, God has the last laugh. This truth is evident in both the Bible and history. Love always wins.

We should not lose heart when it appears that the wicked are prevailing. We can be confident that God will have the final word and His justice will prevail.

The only chance the wicked have is to repent and surrender before it is too late. God has a divine plan and purpose, and nothing the devil does can stop it!

Proverbs 13:18

As I sat behind bars, I couldn't help but notice the revolving door of women coming in and out of the prison system. It was a sad sight to see familiar faces returning time and time again, their potential wasted, and their lives seemingly stuck in a never-ending cycle of crime and punishment. I often wondered what led them back to their old ways, and if there was anything I could do to help break the pattern.

I found solace in prayer, hoping that these women would find the strength and courage to make better choices and turn their lives around. Some of them seemed to have lost everything with each return, while others seemed to have a newfound sense of determination and purpose. It became clear to me that the key to breaking free from the cycle of incarceration was discipline and a willingness to learn from past mistakes.

I witnessed firsthand the transformative power of self-reflection and personal growth. Those who embraced their freedom and took responsibility for their actions were able to flourish and create a new life for themselves. It was a powerful reminder that our choices have the power to shape our future, and that with determination and perseverance, we can overcome even the most challenging circumstances.

December 5

Job 26:6

God's omnipotence knows no bounds, not even the depths of Hell can escape His gaze. Every corner of existence, even beyond time itself, is fully exposed to the Creator.

This truth extends to the realm of the dead as well. There is no limit to where God's power can reach.

While we may face challenges and hardships in life, remember that there is nothing too dark or chaotic for the Lord to transform.

He remains in control at all times. Even when we feel lost, God sees the path ahead clearly. He is the way forward, capable of creating opportunities where none seem to exist.

Our struggles are temporary, and when we bring our sorrows, prayers, and fears to Him, we can find peace.

Whether His response is immediate or deferred, have faith and trust that an answer is already on its way.

December 6

2 Kings 18:6

When faced with challenging situations, our instinct is to seek the quickest and easiest way out or simply give up altogether.

Juggling our daily responsibilities already fills our plates, so adding extra stress can feel overwhelming. However, there is value in persevering, standing firm, and pushing through adversity.

Turning back or straying from the path before us only hinders our progress. Trusting in the Lord during tough times is akin to grasping onto a lifebuoy until we reach the safety of the boat and solid ground.

Initially, holding onto the lifebuoy may seem effortless, but maintaining that grip until reaching the boat can be tiring and frightening. Yet, by not letting go, we are eventually rescued and brought to safety.

We must continue to hold fast to the Lord, even with tired arms, follow His guidance, and have faith that we will reach a place of blessings and security.

1 Chronicles 4:10

There's a popular saying that goes, "A closed mouth doesn't get fed." We have a limited time on Earth to make the most of life and give our best. So, why not be courageous in your prayers when you present them to God?

We often miss out on blessings simply because we fail to ask for them. God blesses us not because we deserve it, but because He can, and because He wants to.

God will always provide us with what draws us closer to Him and glorifies His name, but it will be in His perfect timing, ensuring that we are prepared to receive His blessings.

Welcome God into your heart today. Present all your requests to Him with thanksgiving and seek His guidance to prepare you for the blessings that are headed your way.

In addition, inquire of the Lord how you can bring joy to Him and to those around you while you eagerly anticipate the fulfillment of your blessings in your life.

Psalms 146:7-8

Our God is a compassionate and just God who uses His righteousness and grace to bring about justice. The Bible is full of stories of His deliverance, intervention, healing, and protection.

He delivered His people from oppression and guided them to the promised land. He provided manna when His people were hungry.

He releases prisoners from the sins that bind them, and He lifts up those who are bowed down before Him. He loves, supports, and cares for all those who are His.

Our needs and cries are not hidden from Him. He hears and sees us. He is our God who not only frees us from physical bondage, but also from spiritual bondage.

When God sets us free, it is a call to action to use our experience with Him, as well as our resources, talents, and connections, to help others find freedom through the Lord as well. It's the gift that keeps on giving.

Mark 16:16

This passage has led to much confusion regarding the requirements for salvation. However, when we consider the entirety of God's word and examine all the verses on salvation, it becomes clear that it is only through the grace of Jesus Christ.

If salvation also required water, then the sacrifice on the cross would not have been sufficient. Baptism serves as a beautiful symbol of our faith, signifying our cleansing and rebirth into a new life.

The latter part of this passage emphasizes that those who do not believe will face condemnation. Therefore, faith is essential for salvation - faith in Jesus Christ. Baptism is merely a public declaration of that faith.

The Bible instructs us to spread the gospel worldwide so that others may also believe and be saved. Remember, salvation comes through grace by faith, not by our own works.

John 1:12

Our internal dialogue and the opinions of others can significantly impact our lives. There are moments when we may find ourselves scrutinizing our reflection, mentally listing the aspects we wish were different, or when others may highlight what they perceive as flaws in us.

However, our true value is not determined by such superficial considerations. Upon accepting Jesus Christ as our Lord, we are adopted as children of God, becoming invaluable in His eyes. No material wealth can compare to the worth we hold in God's heart.

He sees us with unconditional love, viewing us as His beloved creations. Therefore, when faced with self-criticism or external negativity, remember that our true value lies in God's love for us, and He loves us just the way we are.

Romans 13:12

When we wake up in the morning and prepare for the day, we are reminded by God to put on His armor. This armor serves as a protective shield that helps us withstand the attacks of the enemy.

As children of the Most High God, we are covered in the blood of Jesus, which means we are fully protected by God's grace. In addition to this, we should also put on the armor of light, and behave as children of God who carry His name.

Putting on the armor of God is essentially clothing ourselves with Him. Ephesians explains the different aspects of the armor of God, with each piece representing a different aspect of who He is.

God is truth, righteousness, peace, salvation, and the sword that we can use against the enemy's attacks. Our faith comes from Him and serves as our shield to protect us from Satan's attacks.

We have been given everything we need to win every battle, but it's up to us to wake up every day and put on the armor of God Himself, shining His light to overcome the darkness ahead.

December 12

2 Corinthians 1:5

There are Christians worldwide who face persecution daily due to their faith in Jesus Christ. You may have also experienced persecution yourself.

I have personally encountered various forms of persecution since dedicating my life to the Lord, but I have learned to embrace it as part of the journey.

It is not to be unexpected, as the Bible forewarns us about such trials. Our duty is to endure as Christ did, seeking comfort in God amidst the challenges we encounter.

Following Jesus' example, we should pray for our enemies, hoping that God will lead them to repentance before it is too late.

We should also pray for God's deliverance during times of adversity, expressing gratitude for His blessings and presence as we remain steadfast in our faith, confronting those who oppose Him.

December 13

John 14:27

Encountering someone with a gun can be a terrifying situation. It's much riskier to face someone who is fearful and reactive, compared to someone who is calm and collected due to training.

Living in fear can lead to hasty decisions and mistakes. God doesn't want us to be consumed by fear. Making choices out of fear often results in a chain of poor decisions.

The Lord provides us with peace through His love, sacrifice, and teachings. By trusting in Him, we can make wise choices and find peace in any circumstance. This requires faith, but it leads to victory.

The temporary offerings of the world pale in comparison to the transformative peace that comes from Christ, guiding us away from worldly worries and into His comforting rest.

Matthew 22:37-38

This scripture is Jesus' response to a question about the most important commandment, and it should serve as the cornerstone of our lives.

The foundation of everything we do is based on our relationship with God. All aspects of our lives revolve around the commitment and effort we put into making God the main priority.

Love is simple, but people tend to complicate things by placing value in meaningless pursuits. By allowing love to guide our lives, we can center our families, homes, decisions, and hearts around it.

Love is the ultimate perfection, as God Himself is love. We are created in His image to have an intimate relationship with Him, reflecting the same love He shows us.

Consider what God sacrificed to demonstrate His love - His only son. What are you willing to sacrifice for Him? He is deserving of our love and adoration, as He gives us His best. Turn to God today and let Him know how much He means to you.

December 15

Psalms 7:1

When we align ourselves with God, we automatically become adversaries of the devil. We are caught in the midst of the eternal struggle between good and evil. However, we are not left to fight alone.

We are chosen by God, vessels of His Holy Spirit. The power of God resides within us. When it seems like the enemy is too strong, or the battle is lost, we simply need to turn inward and pray, calling out to God for deliverance from our foes while seeking comfort in His embrace. Victory over our adversaries will always come from God.

David, who had a deep connection with the Lord and was a man after God's own heart, placed unwavering trust in God and withheld nothing from Him. David faced numerous challenges, confronted enemies, and encountered dangers, yet he laid everything before the Lord because he understood that only God could guide him safely through.

Regardless of the obstacles we encounter or the size of the opposition, our God is in control, and He will grant us victory according to His divine plan as long as we place our faith in Him.

Romans 1:5

Grace is the core of God's heart and the essence of the gospel. The term grace is mentioned more than 150 times in the Bible, signifying its immense importance.

It is a gift freely given to us through the sacrifice and blood of Jesus Christ. This precious gift is not something we could ever earn, but it is bestowed upon us because of God's love for us, not because of our own merit.

Grace is a powerful force that enables us to fulfill our purpose and is something we can freely share with others. It is a force of love that extends its own power. When we accept this grace, we become living testimonies of God's power in our lives, demonstrating our faith.

Our stories and personal encounters with God can lead others to the cross. God has a story to share through us, and we have a story to share through God.

The world needs to hear these stories of hope, redemption, and triumph over adversity so that they too can experience the hope found in our Lord Jesus.

December 17

1 Corinthians 6:11

The devil is the great accuser, always trying to highlight your past mistakes and doing whatever he can to divert attention from who you are now - a completely forgiven, and completely loved child of God. We are all well aware of who we were in the past, we don't need any reminding. That's why we must keep looking forward at the road ahead, and not at what's behind us.

Looking in the rearview mirror while driving the whole time will only cause you to wreck. You must stay focused. You have been washed clean from all the dirt of your past and set apart for good, justified by the name of Jesus and the Spirit of our Most High God. Satan can accuse all he wants, but his opinion amounts to nothing.

Only the opinion of our loving Lord matters, and He is doing everything He can to get you to see yourself through His grace filled eyes and heart, because He knows once you do, you will stop letting the devil get in your ear trying to convince you otherwise.

Celebrate the fulness of God's love in your life today and allow His voice to be the only voice that guides you through this journey called life.

December 18

2 Chronicles 32:7-8

As believers, we are engaged in a constant battle. The enemy never gives up. He may know he's defeated in the end, but he's determined to cause as much damage as possible along the way.

There will be moments in life where we feel trapped with no way out. We will encounter situations that seem impossible to overcome, but in those times, there's one thing we can do. Instead of endlessly searching for answers, we can turn to the one who holds all the cards - our Heavenly Father.

When we come face to face with opposition from the world, remember that the world relies on its own limited resources. We, on the other hand, have access to God's unlimited power to defeat worldly forces. Just look at the countless victories God has granted His people in the Bible when they faced unbeatable enemies.

Stay strong in your faith and be brave, for God is with you, mighty warrior.

December 19

John 9:11

Jesus has the ability to look deep within us and understand our true selves in a way that the world cannot comprehend. The key to knowing one another is by spending time together. While the world may judge based on appearances, God does not.

It's easy for the world to make assumptions about a homeless man begging for food, but the truth may be that he is a wounded veteran who has lost his family and is struggling to find his way. We cannot assume to understand someone's heart and life based on brief encounters; we must take the time to get to know them.

In this scripture, Jesus healed a man's disability to reveal God's power. While God doesn't have to work in such ways to reveal Himself, there is much to be learned when He does.

Jesus didn't just say "be healed" and have the man instantly cured; he used worldly resources, gave the man directions to follow, and the man followed in faith and was healed. God wants us to have faith and open our eyes to the healing He has waiting for us.

December 20

Romans 12:15

We were designed for fellowship. To be a part of the body and family of Christ. When one part of the body is happy, we all share in that joy, and when one part is in pain, the rest of the body steps in to provide care. The entire body is affected by the suffering of one part or the blessing that is received.

When someone stands by our side to offer their compassion and encouragement, we may not recall their words, but we remember how they made us feel and that they were there for us. God understands the significance of presence, which is why He emphasizes His omnipresence in the Bible.

This assures us that we are not alone in our triumphs or our struggles. We just need to be attentive and empathetic to what our fellow brothers and sisters are experiencing, so that we can support each other with love, compassion, understanding, and encouragement.

December 21

1 Corinthians 15:57

If you watch sports, you understand the pivotal role the team's coach plays in determining the outcome of a game and even the entire season.

The coach provides instructions, and it is the team's commitment to following those instructions that can ultimately lead them to victory. In life, Jesus not only serves as our coach but also as a player who revolutionized the game.

He accomplished what no one else could, and now we have the privilege of looking up to Him, receiving guidance from Him, and rejoicing in our victory because of Him!

Every day, we step onto the field of life as we rise out of bed. We strive towards the goal line, rallying our teammates for support when faced with tough opposition.

Our actions reflect our coach, who stands by us, offering love, encouragement, and direction as we navigate the game. Let us express gratitude to our Savior today, who always leads us to victory!

December 22

Matthew 12:48-50

Who does the Lord consider to be His family? According to these verses, anyone who follows the will of God is considered family by Him. Our relationships with those who draw us closer to the Lord are more important than our worldly relationships.

They help us strengthen our bond with God and feel His presence in our lives. The only blood that matters in terms of family is the blood of Jesus Christ. The Bible mentions that some may lose relationships with their worldly family due to their faith in Jesus (Luke 21:16-18 and Matthew 10:35-39.) However, they will not be left alone.

God has given us a new family of believers who share our faith. This doesn't mean we should abandon our worldly families if they are not believers, but rather that we should always prioritize the Lord's will over our family's desires.

So, even if your earthly family rejects you, remember that you have a family in Christ who will always welcome you with love and acceptance, pleasing our Heavenly Father.

December 23

2 Corinthians 5:1

From the moment of our birth, our bodies begin the natural process of aging, ultimately leading to our final breath. These bodies we inhabit are not designed to last forever.

Throughout our lives, we will inevitably face suffering, illness, and pain. However, there is a light at the end of the tunnel! The Holy Spirit residing within us has sealed us with a promise.

Our eternal home in Heaven awaits us, with our names written on it. Although we may currently be walking through the valley of the shadow of death, we need not fear, for the Lord our God is by our side, supporting us, and has already prepared for what is to come.

Our physical bodies may falter, life may disappoint us, and even our loved ones may let us down, but the Lord remains faithful. He fulfills every promise He makes, offering us peace and assurance for the future, knowing that Heaven is our everlasting home where suffering will be no more.

December 24

John 7:24

Jesus has called us to make righteous judgements, not judging others or situations by the world's terms. We are supposed to use sound judgement according to the values, principles, and commandments that God has given to us. We should be asking ourselves many times a day, "what would Jesus do?"

In order to make sound judgements we really have to get into the word of God and see how He has worked through the lives of others and know His commandments and what is expected of us. We have a huge responsibility, with great reward on the way. We can't look at things from a fleshly perspective and expect to make a good judgement about it.

We can't merely look at a box and call it a box alone when there's so much more it contains inside. We have to open it up and see what contents it holds. We also need to reflect on the standards in which we hold others. Are we holding them to a higher standard than we are for ourselves?

Jesus is the standard in which we all must strive to become like. So, let us reflect on our hearts and lives, and make sure we're doing everything we can to get them in alignment with the heart of God.

Romans 12:17

This passage challenges our natural instincts. When we are wronged, our first impulse is often to seek revenge and make the other person suffer.

However, God reminds us that vengeance is His alone (Romans 12:19). He understands that responding with anger and hostility will only lead to more pain for ourselves and those around us.

It is crucial to exercise self-control and set a positive example for others. As representatives of God, we must conduct ourselves in a manner that reflects His character.

Just think, if God treated us with the punishment we deserve instead of showing us grace, where would we be? Therefore, we are called to extend grace to others, even when it goes against our very nature.

Let us emulate Jesus' example by spreading love and forgiveness, rather than contributing to the cycle of hatred and suffering in the world.

December 26

Matthew 23:12

Jesus, the son of God who sits at the right hand of His Father, exemplifies true humility. He did not come to Earth to flaunt His achievements or divine status. Instead, He approached His mission with humility, using His position to bring healing change to the world.

Despite holding the highest position alongside His Father in Heaven, He willingly took on the role of a servant. Jesus never made others feel unworthy of approaching Him; He met people where they were and worked tirelessly to uplift them.

He always acknowledged the source of His power and blessings, giving credit to His Father in Heaven. His ultimate goal was to fulfill the work assigned to Him by pleasing His Father.

Just as Jesus did, we should cultivate humility in our attitudes. If we must boast, let it be in the Lord, recognizing that all good things come from above, not through our own efforts or abilities.

December 27

1 Corinthians 12:27

We were never meant to go through life alone. No one person can handle everything on their own. We are designed to collaborate as a team.

A tailor may not have the expertise to construct a house from scratch like a builder would, and vice versa. Each of us possesses unique skills that come together to strengthen the community as a whole.

We are like individual puzzle pieces that, when placed together, form a beautiful picture. While one piece may not show the full image, it is vital in completing it.

Let's embrace the joy of our work today, contributing to God's vision coming to life. Despite our unique talents, we all serve the same loving God. May we work with love and for His honor.

December 28

John 14:1

Anxiety is a common struggle that many of us face. When challenges arise, it's natural to feel overwhelmed, but Jesus encourages us to place our trust in Him, despite the fears that may consume us.

Although we may not physically see God, rest assured that He is always by your side. Even when we can't predict the future, God knows what lies ahead and He always brings about good for those who have faith in Him.

Jesus didn't give us a step-by-step guide for our lives, but He extends His hand to lead us through the darkness of this world. He is our ultimate source of strength and guidance, providing us with everything we need to reach our final destination. There's no need to waste time worrying about the unknown when we have Jesus by our side.

By knowing Jesus, we also come to know the Father who sent Him, making God's love and care our own. We are embraced by the heart of Jesus, which is at the core of our Father's boundless love for us.

December 29

Romans 8:28

On my way to begin serving my seven-year prison sentence, I was completely unaware of how God could turn any good out of the situation, or out of the chaos that had consumed my life up to that point. I couldn't fathom having anything to look forward to, except for the stigma of being a felon and the remorse of hurting and losing time with my loved ones.

Surprisingly, God used that moment, along with all the struggles leading up to it, as a pivotal moment in my life that ultimately led to redemption and renewal. During my time in prison, I found Jesus as my Savior and God as my compassionate Father.

He shattered the chains of addiction that once bound me and severed toxic relationships. He restored broken relationships with faith and lifted the weight of guilt from my shoulders.

Additionally, the Lord brought new, healthy relationships into my life and has used me in various ways to shine His light and display His greatness. Never underestimate the power of God to transform the darkness in your life. The darker the night, the brighter the dawn.

December 30

Isaiah 43:12

God's power is evident in the miracles He performs in our lives, the ways He provides for us, and the strength He gives us to overcome challenges. His mercy is displayed in His forgiveness and compassion towards us, despite our shortcomings and sins. And His authority is displayed in His control over all things, including our lives and the world around us.

Through His grace, God has saved us from eternal separation from Him and has given us the opportunity to have a relationship with Him. It is important to remember that it is not our own efforts or abilities that have saved us, but rather God's love and sacrifice for us.

As believers, we are called to be witnesses and share our testimonies of God's saving grace with others, so that they too may come to know Him and experience His love.

As we await the return of Jesus, let us continue to support and encourage one another in our faith. Let us hold fast to God as our one true source of salvation and trust in His plan for our lives. May we always remember the incredible gift of grace that God has given us and share that gift with others.

December 31

Revelation 3:21

We are faced with a single decision in this lifetime, and it is the only decision that matters. We must either choose to accept Jesus as our Savior or reject Him. It's as straightforward as that. Every subsequent choice we make reflects that pivotal decision. For those of us who sincerely choose Him, follow Him, and understand His heart, we will have the privilege of sitting with Jesus on His throne, just as He triumphed and sat down with His Father.

We will have the ability to conquer the world and all the obstacles the devil has placed in our path to bring about our downfall. We will rejoice in our victory alongside Jesus and our Father for all eternity. Our task on Earth is to put on the spiritual armor of God, remain steadfast in our faith, and anticipate the glory that lies ahead.

We possess the power and authority of God to reign and achieve victory over all challenges and adversaries that seek to harm us. Through our compassionate Savior, we will participate in this victory and eternal joy! Let us give praise to our God, who has enabled us to overcome sin and share in the throne with Christ our Lord in the Heavenly Kingdom that awaits us.

Made in the USA
Monee, IL
09 September 2024

65334642R10224